T0043294

For my money, Object Lessons is the most consistently interesting nonfiction book series in America."

Megan Volpert, *PopMatters*

Besides being beautiful little hand-sized objects themselves, showcasing exceptional writing, the wonder of these books is that they exist at all . . . Uniformly excellent, engaging, thought-provoking, and informative."

Jennifer Bort Yacovissi, *Washington Independent Review of Books*

. . . edifying and entertaining . . . perfect for slipping in a pocket and pulling out when life is on hold."

Sarah Murdoch, *Toronto Star*

[W]itty, thought-provoking, and poetic . . . These little books are a page-flipper's dream."

John Timpane, *The Philadelphia Inquirer*

Though short, at roughly 25,000 words apiece, these books are anything but slight."

Marina Benjamin, *New Statesman*

The joy of the series, of reading *Remote Control,*
Golf Ball, Driver's License, Drone, Silence, Glass,
Refrigerator, Hotel, and *Waste* . . . in quick succession,
lies in encountering the various turns through which
each of their authors has been put by his or her object.
. . . The object predominates, sits squarely center stage,
directs the action. The object decides the genre, the
chronology, and the limits of the study. Accordingly,
the author has to take her cue from the *thing* she chose
or that chose her. The result is a wonderfully uneven
series of books, each one a *thing* unto itself."

Julian Yates, *Los Angeles Review of Books*

The Object Lessons series has a beautifully simple
premise. Each book or essay centers on a specific
object. This can be mundane or unexpected, humorous
or politically timely. Whatever the subject, these
descriptions reveal the rich worlds hidden under the
surface of things."

Christine Ro, *Book Riot*

. . . a sensibility somewhere between Roland Barthes and
Wes Anderson."

Simon Reynolds, author of *Retromania: Pop*
Culture's Addiction to Its Own Past

OBJECT LESSONS

A book series about the hidden lives of ordinary things.

Series Editors:

Ian Bogost and Christopher Schaberg

In association with

BOOKS IN THE SERIES

stroller

AMANDA PARRISH MORGAN

BLOOMSBURY ACADEMIC
NEW YORK · LONDON · OXFORD · NEW DELHI · SYDNEY

BLOOMSBURY ACADEMIC
Bloomsbury Publishing Inc
1385 Broadway, New York, NY 10018, USA
50 Bedford Square, London, WC1B 3DP, UK
29 Earlsfort Terrace, Dublin 2, Ireland

BLOOMSBURY, BLOOMSBURY ACADEMIC and the Diana logo are trademarks
of Bloomsbury Publishing Plc

First published in the United States of America 2022
Reprinted 2023

Cover design: Alice Marwick

Library of Congress Cataloging-in-Publication Data

Names: Parrish Morgan, Amanda, author.
Title: Stroller / Amanda Parrish Morgan.
Description: 1st Edition. | New York : Bloomsbury Academic, [2022] | Series: Object lessons |
Includes bibliographical references and index. | Summary: "Through memoir, historical research,
and cultural criticism, Stroller explores what this ubiquitous baby equipment reveals about our
attitudes toward parenthood and children"– Provided by publisher.
Identifiers: LCCN 2022009687 (print) | LCCN 2022009688 (ebook) | ISBN 9781501386664
(paperback) | ISBN 9781501386671 (epub) | ISBN 9781501386688 (pdf) | ISBN 9781501386695
Subjects: LCSH: Baby strollers–Social aspects. | Parenthood. | Children.
Classification: LCC GT2468 .P37 2022 (print) | LCC GT2468 (ebook) |
DDC 392.1/3–dc23/eng/20220519
LC record available at https://lccn.loc.gov/2022009687
LC ebook record available at https://lccn.loc.gov/2022009688

ISBN: PB: 978-1-5013-8666-4
ePDF: 978-1-5013-8668-8
eBook: 978-1-5013-8667-1

Series: Object Lessons

Typeset by Deanta Global Publishing Services, Chennai, India
Printed and bound in Great Britain

To find out more about our authors and books visit www.bloomsbury.com and sign up for our
newsletters.

for Thea and Simon

CONTENTS

FIGURES

A TAXONOMY OF STROLLERS

1. One who strolls
   a. who walks in a leisurely or idle manner
   b. who goes from place to place in search of work or profit
2. Baby commodity
   a. Umbrella stroller: lightweight, collapsible, relatively inexpensive and portable (often fits in the overheard compartment on an airplane) wheeled carriage for a seated baby
   b. Pram: short for *perambulator*; a flat bassinet on four wheels in which a baby can ride while lying down (and as a result, unlike many other strollers, is safe for newborns)

    c. Travel system: separate parts (for example a car seat, a wheeled frame, a collapsible stroller) that can be assembled in various combinations

    d. In-line stroller: tandem seating for multiples or young children close in age

    e. Side-by-side stroller: seating for up to three children straight across

    f. Running stroller: lightweight (often aluminum) frame, oversize wheels, adjustable handle grip OR in some newer models pulled with a harness, behind the runner to allow for more natural running form

3. Near-strollers

    a. Bike trailer: lightweight carriage pulled behind a bicycle, usually accommodates one or two children

    b. Stroll-N-Trike: a tricycle with a long handle allowing a child to pedal or be pushed from behind by a parent

    c. Toddler Push Car: a low-to-the ground plastic car with a long handle allowing a single child to ride, as in a typical stroller

d. Shopping cart: with seating for one, two, or three children (officially), sometimes shaped like plastic cars or fire engines

e. Doll stroller or pram: plastic, wooden or metal; in some cases, sturdy enough for an older child to push a younger sibling (precariously)

4. Stroller as Metaphor

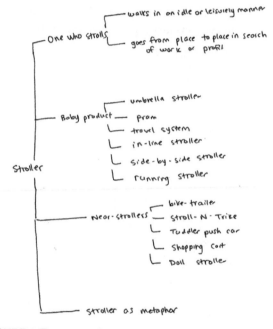

FIGURE 1 Taxonomy of strollers.

1 WHAT TO EXPECT

A few weeks after I got married, I had dinner with the woman I then considered my closest friend. We sat next to a floor-to-ceiling window, and I spent most of the meal shredding my napkin under the table. Ann had never explicitly told me she found women with children to be a combination of pitiable, irritating, and boring, but I understood this because I had once agreed. Or in some ways still did agree. Together we'd rolled our eyes at Christmas cards with sonogram images, or at the parents—almost always mothers—who came to the high school where we taught to deliver missing homework assignments or request meetings about their children's academic achievement. I'd spent most of my twenties sensing generally that there was something embarrassing, especially for women, about wanting to have children. It involved a shameful combination of lack of ambition and the worst cliches of conformity and femininity.

"I think Nick and I are going to try to have a baby," I said. I laughed in the uncomfortable way and darted my eyes back and forth from her face to the glass of wine I was drinking.

"That'll be the end of all your running," she said and laughed a short, hard syllable.

I started running competitively when I was 14 and had stopped for an extended period—six weeks to let a pair of tibial stress fractures heal—just once. A few months before dinner with Ann, I'd raced my fifth marathon. I was teaching English and coaching the cross country and track teams at a public high school just a few miles away from the town where I grew up. Being a runner—not just running for exercise, but training daily and competing in races year in and year out—was as much a part of who I was as being a teacher or a writer, and at that point, more a part of who I was than being married or hoping to be a mother.

I'd thought a lot about how my life would change if I had children. I'd thought anxiously about the possibility of a high-risk pregnancy or the challenges of raising a child with extraordinary medical or emotional needs. Nick and I had considered the possibilities for work and childcare. I worried about infertility and birth injuries and breastfeeding struggles. I had annotated my district's family leave policy. I worried I'd gain weight I'd never lose. I worried I might be very tired or my house might be very dirty. I'd even worried that my race times would be slower. But I hadn't thought to worry that I might lose the steady, reliable joy of running itself. In college our assistant coach had run with us well into her third trimester of pregnancy and then resumed running with us just a few weeks after delivering her son. I already knew we'd get a jogging stroller which I imagined as piece of equipment that would make it possible not to give up running, but simply to adapt it to include a baby.

But of course, underlying Ann's flippant response was the same fundamental truth that lay beneath all the fears I had privately acknowledged: my life was going to change irrevocably, consequentially, and unpredictably in ways that would make me unrecognizable to myself. Running, as she and I both knew, was shorthand for my autonomy; the luxury of dedicating time to pursue that, while serious and life-long, were ultimately non-essential. My body would change, maybe forever. My friendships would change. Some, like mine with Ann, with whom I'd traveled across state lines to race half-marathons and shared thousands of miles worth of training and conversation, would end.

My daughter Thea was born twelve days past her due date, on a late December morning, just ten months after that dinner. I went for a run-walk that morning, hoping to finally kick-start labor and with a defiant and defensive relief as I waddle-jogged the half-mile from the town playground to our driveway: pregnancy, at least, had not been an end to all my running.

Nick and I didn't have a baby shower. All that accumulation of stuff felt embarrassing. I'd seen and ridiculed the cakes made to look like pregnant women, games involving melted candy bars in diapers, bows placed on round bellies. And we were very lucky. My parents and in-laws generously gave us much of what I absurdly thought we needed: six different animal hooded bath towels; a crib and changing table; a lamp with a porcelain elephant base that ended up shattered on the floor; and a $500 jogging stroller.

I had imagined I'd start to use the stroller as soon as I was running again after delivery. I knew so little about babies, though, that I hadn't realized that infants can't ride in a running stroller without an attachment to secure a rear-facing car seat above the regular stroller seat until around six months, when they have enough neck control to sit up on their own.

So, instead, on days when the temperature was above freezing, I took Thea on slow walks zig-zagging through our neighborhood in something called a "travel system." This three-piece set looked very confusing when I ordered it, but using it quickly became simple and essential. It consisted of an infant car seat, a base to install in the car, and a stroller-frame that the seat could snap in and out of without unclipping or even moving the baby. If Thea fell asleep on the drive home from the pediatrician's office, I could unsnap the infant seat and carry it into the living room where she would nap while I wrote or did a load of laundry or staggered exhaustedly to sleep on the couch next to her.

By the spring, when Thea was strong enough for the running stroller, I had gone back to work coaching high schoolers. I'd started running with them, which required using my double-electric breast pump in the car just before practice and carefully storing the expressed milk on ice in a little cooler and then changing into two sports bras to support my swollen breasts. Some days it was impossible for

FIGURE 2 Thea in pink fleece in stroller.

me to run at practice: the team had a meet or was doing hard intervals that I timed, or I needed to monitor injured runners cross training in the fitness center.

These were the days I'd wanted the stroller for. I'd imagined, correctly, that even knowing I had the option to get fresh air and a dose of endorphins would be reassuring. A reminder that, if I were willing to think strategically about timing and nursing and pumping, and push thirty pounds of stroller and baby while I did it, I could be a mother and a runner at the same time. That caregiving and ambition were not mutually exclusive.

2 BABY PRODUCTS AND BABIES AS PRODUCTS

The school year when my daughter, Thea, was four and my son, Simon, was two, I dropped them off and later picked them up at different times from different preschools. The most efficient way to do this was to run pushing them both in the double jogging stroller I got for Christmas just five days before Simon was born. This way I could get a run in and drop them off or pick them up, in only a minute or two more than it would have taken to get them in their car seats, unload first at Thea's school, then reload Simon in the car, take him to his preschool, and drive back home. If I did it all on foot, I could drop them off, jog home pushing the empty stroller and frantically write a few pages before starting the second half of my run a few hours later when it was time to pick them up.

However efficient, this routine also meant I was often sweaty, late, and at least twice each day running down the street pushing an empty double stroller. Well-meaning neighbors made jokes I hated, especially in the blocks between preschools when only one seat of the double stroller was occupied. ("You lost one!") and other runners sometimes shouted encouragement ("go, Mama" was most common) or made oddly self-deprecating yet competitive remarks if I overtook them while pushing the stroller ("You're making me look bad" and once, a straightforward "this is humiliating" from a not-particularly-fit-looking man about my age). Even in the moments I was standing outside one of their preschools—places full of young children and the accessories used to transport them—I never completely shook a sense of self-consciousness over my sweaty face, my heavy breathing, or the slight smell I knew the stroller and I both must be giving off.

Around me, other caretakers—mostly mothers, but also a few fathers and nannies—pushed sleek urban strollers, like the UPPABaby VISTA, which comes with a removable bassinet ($1229.98 including car seat, $929.99 without) or its double iteration ($1149.97, no car seat option) and its attendant accessories: the Carryall Parent Organizer ($34.99), the Snack Tray ($39.99), the Cozy Ganoosh Footmuff ($149.99) or the Ride-Along Board ($119.99), a wheeled platform designed for children too old to ride in a stroller but too young for a full-day's walking (uppababy .com). It's possible I was just imagining that these strollers were cleaner than mine, their crevices less coated with crumbs, their fabric less stained with spilled milk, their sun canopies less mildewed from being folded away while still damp—but they all looked immaculate. It's also possible that, although this running stroller commute made me feel more accomplished, and in that sense more put-together than I would have otherwise, the physical evidence that I did not have time to separate exercising from commuting from parenting felt like something of a public failure. Even now, years removed from the time when I had only four hours each week in which both kids were at school, I don't know what I'd have done differently: this arrangement was what worked best for our family, and in the end it mostly worked out for me to run and parent and commute simultaneously and write in stolen moments. I'd likely never have been the kind of person with a clean stroller, no matter its brand or the number of hours a week of childcare I had.

At one point we owned five strollers: a single running stroller, a double running stroller, an easily collapsible umbrella stroller, the perplexing-turned-second-nature travel system, and a hand-me-down stroller designed to allow one child to ride facing forward and another to easily hop on and off. All of them, even those that we'd received in excellent condition, were untidy. The strollers, their accessories and condition, were markers of other things. In the same way that certain makes and models of cars, the presence of a Little Free Library or an NPR tote bag can signal a whole set of economic and cultural alliances, strollers do the same.

The four-figure UPPABaby VISTA strollers, popular among the recently transplanted suburbanites in my town, are high-end, but far from the most outrageously expensive on the market. Fendi makes a baby stroller (listed for $3290.00 on farfetch.com) and the storied English brand, Silver Cross, whose designs look largely unchanged since their debut in the Edwardian era sells a pram called "Balmoral" for $3999.99 (free shipping, though). *Town and Country* reported that this model was Kate Middleton's stroller of choice (Silverman).

The first perambulator (or pram for short) was invented by William Kent in 1733 for the Duke and Duchess of Devonshire, and it was designed to be pulled by a goat. In 1923, Samuel Sewell gave a very solemn and comprehensive history of British pram innovation, "Children's and Invalids' Carriages," at the 21st ordinary meeting of the Royal Society of the Arts. The society's journal published a transcript of Sewell's talk and the debate that followed it (which, apparently, was neither as vigorous nor as rigorous as Sewell had hoped). Sewell bemoans the paucity of scholarship on the history of prams and the terminology used for the objects: "[s]uch vehicles are generally called perambulators or bassinettes. That nomenclature is, I must admit, unsatisfactory since the name comes from *per* and *ambulare,* meaning to walk through or over and thus it is the person who wheels the vehicle who is the perambulator according to our best dictionaries and not the carriage itself" (Sewell 716).

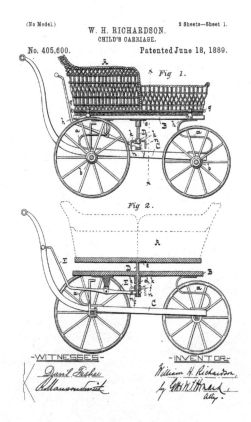

W. H. RICHARDSON.
CHILD'S CARRIAGE.

No. 405,600.

Patented June 18, 1889.

Fig 1.

Fig 2.

-WITNESSES-

Dan'l Fisher

-INVENTOR-

William H. Richardson,

FIGURE 3 Patent for Richardson's stroller.

Sewell explains that although William Kent's goat-pulled baby carriage was the first of its kind in Britain, earlier versions appeared in ancient cultures from Athens to Japan. His talk details different technological innovations across cultures and centuries. By the time Charles Burton received the first British patent for a perambulator in 1853, his model had evolved from the four-wheeled type invented by Kent to a design that looks more like contemporary strollers with only three wheels. In subsequent years, the invention was improved by advances, like William Richardson's reversible bassinet. Later, the introduction of features for comfort like springs and upholstery, or restraints, breaking mechanisms,

Major Russell Harrison and Harrison children outside the White House, 1890

FIGURE 4 Goat pulling Harrison's child in stroller.

FIGURE 5 Woman pushing gas-safe pram.

and lowering the center of gravity made prams safer. The Victoria and Albert Museum displays wicker prams, wooden prams, double prams, reversible prams. An iconic, macabre Getty photograph shows two women in gas masks pushing a gas-safe pram through the streets of Kingston in 1941.

In the remarks he made to the Royal Society, more than a decade before the photograph of the gas-safe pram, Sewell claimed "that for the first-born even the poorest mother insists on a new pram, and that she wants one different from her neighbors" (720). Not just different, it would seem, but safer, as illustrated by his subsequent offhanded list of "numerous accidents" in which children have injured themselves in prams—flipping over, falling out, rolling away—"sometimes with fatal results" (Sewell 724). What item could be more worthy of investment than one designed to ensure the comfort and safety—maybe even the survival—of an infant?

When Thea was a toddler and I was pregnant with Simon, we spent a sweltering summer weekend in Manhattan. After an early wake up, croissants, and coffee, we wandered to a large, shaded playground in TriBeCa, a wealthy neighborhood that John Freeman Gill profiled in a 2011 Real Estate piece for the *New York Times* with a headline calling it "The Land of the $800 Stroller," and a place where urban legend says it's common practice to employ not just a nanny but also a reading tutor and a math tutor and a private yoga instructor, all before kindergarten, to ensure successful preschool admission. We parked our stroller in the shade at the far east side of the playground, and unclipped untutored-suburban-public-school-bound Thea.

I tried to strike the right balance between hovering and supervising. In between stretches of holding her hand while she tried the slide and reminding her not to eat sand, I returned to a bench next to where our stroller was lined up alongside dozens of others. Ours was clearly the wrong kind. Our Mountain Buggy Terrain running stroller was too big for city streets and much too dirty for TriBeCa: the dark gray seat streaked with thick white sunscreen and its underneath carrying compartment overstuffed with the diaper bag, snacks for later, and a half-eaten croissant. I'd not yet heard of a Parent Organizer then, but saw most of the other strollers—UPPABaby VISTAS all, it seemed—had one, a tidy place for an iced coffee and a cell phone and a set of keys. It was not the land of $800 strollers, but of $1500 strollers.

Before Thea was born and we were deciding which baby things to buy, I mostly made the decisions on my own, and without a lot of research. I didn't have many of friends with kids yet, and so what research I did do often involved googling things like "best running stroller" and clicking on a few that turned up near the top of a consumer reports list. They all looked the same and, I assumed, worked roughly the same way. But standing off to the side of that playground, I felt like a suburban mother version of the archetypal American tourist my high school French teacher warned us not to embody—white sneakers, map out, camera around our necks as we wandered around Paris. "That stroller costs a thousand dollars," I whispered to Nick, motioning to a model that I now realize I was under-valuing by at least 50 percent.

In the summer of 2000, long before I was pregnant, or knew Nick, or would have even admitted to myself that I'd like to have children someday, Janelle Taylor published "Of Sonograms and Baby Prams" in the "Women and Health" volume of *Feminist Studies*. Her essay makes the case that pregnancy and motherhood had then become framed largely through the lens of consumption and the resulting cultural emphasis on the *production* in *reproduction*. I'd absorbed quite a bit of misogynistic dismissal of mothers without realizing it, and much of that was rooted in the notion that women with young children were easy targets for the notion that parenting was primarily a consumer endeavor rather than an emotional, moral, intellectual, or even spiritual one.

Taylor outlines the ways in which conventional conversations around pregnancy and prenatal testing often have the effect of positioning the doctor as a manager and the mother as an unskilled laborer in the work of producing an ideal, optimized product—the fetus. The idea that a fetus and later a child is a commodity falls neatly in line with some of the most abhorrent parenting trends of recent decades. In communities where parents have the financial resources and access to power, parental interference with the intent to maximize children's "value" plays out in public scandals like "Operation Varsity Blues." Before I had children, though I wouldn't have been able to articulate it, I had this vague sense that because the most visible examples of parenting (good and bad) were done by women, parenting that positions a child—or a fetus—as a product was the fault of women, of mothers. But, Taylor draws an important connection between a society that sees children as products and the associated commodification of the mother herself: "[T]he routinization of prenatal diagnostic technologies has aroused concern from many quarters that embryos and fetuses are being reduced the state of commodities," she explains, adding that "feminists have voiced further concern that women are, in the process, being reduced to the status of unskilled reproductive workers who produce these valued commodities through their alienated labor" (395).

When I was in labor with Thea, astounded both by how much pain I was in and how unprepared I had been for this amount of pain, I thought about the word "delivery" and the responsibility it implied—that I had to deliver her safely from where she'd been to the world outside. I thought about the word "labor," too, in that it required work to be in so much pain, to stay focused on a physically exhausting task for so many hours, but I had not considered the word's other connotation: "human activity that provides the goods or services in an economy."

Viewing a baby as a product, of course, is not a new phenomenon, even if brand-sponsored birth announcements, baby registries full of UPPABaby VISTA accessories, and gender-revealing ultrasounds followed by pink-or-blue-crème-filled-cakes are.

In her research, Taylor examines the role that baby showers have come to play in the commodification of pregnancy and early motherhood. Once primarily a ritual means of conveying wisdom from mothers and grandmothers to expectant mothers, they have instead become almost entirely about consumer goods. We were lucky to have the luxury of finding a baby shower overly-consumer focused; we could afford what we really needed and even that which we'd only been lead to believe we needed (all those hooded animal towels), and I'd not be the first to realize that as a wealthy white woman living in a safe suburb, I have the luxury of pushing a dirty jogging stroller day in and day out for six years and risk only light disdain rather than deeper assumptions about what I might be failing to provide for my children in terms of cleanliness and safety.

Had gender reveal parties been a widely known phenomena in 2000, they, too, would surely have featured as a prime example of what Taylor observes. One ultrasound technician compared expectant parents to "shoppers," focused on the sex of their developing baby to the exclusion of its healthy anatomical development. On the one hand, Taylor admits, the extension of targeted marketing to expectant parents is not so different from the already widespread "phenomenon of parents buying stuff for their kids," something that Americans now accept without question despite the fact that as recently as the early twentieth century, such targeted advertising was considered an intrusion from the "profane world of business into the sacred space of the home" (398). I'm glad that I can buy Trader Joe's meals and baby bottles and laundry detergent—profane intrusions from the world of business—but there's something viscerally romantic and appealing about imagining the walls of our house sheltering my children, if not me and Nick, from the imperative to consume.

"We went to these childbirth classes," one of the women Taylor interviewed remembers, "and they were telling us all these different things you have to buy, and it all just seemed really intimidating. I mean, there's the baby carrier and the breast pump and the stroller and two different kinds of car seats, and I don't know how to even use them" (399). I hadn't known how to use any of these things either. We only had one kind of car seat (should we have had another?) but we had a baby carrier I was too nervous to use for months, a breast pump I didn't understand how to assemble, and of course our various strollers with their specific and particular rules and signals and situational appropriateness.

Sewell's tone is unintentionally hilarious. With a mix of boastful British stroller pride and false modesty about his own presentation, he expresses his dismay that women without means are desiring expensive prams. His dismissiveness and judgement come off as something along the lines of, "Oh those silly ladies have been fooled into buying these contraptions for the sake of appearances." Taylor, by contrast, seems determined to avoid casting unfair judgement on the women she interviews. But they are both driving toward a common truth: that the marketing of baby goods as synonymous with attentive parenting is driving the consumption of those goods.

In a world inclined to see a child as a commodity and to frame spending for and around pregnancy and childbirth as an "investment," even decisions that don't deal explicitly with purchasing products or services for children are often framed as issues of consumer choice and as a means of constructing an identity that runs parallel to the way high-end baby purchases do. The attitude described by the ultrasound technician where parents viewed themselves as shoppers might apply to decisions about pain management during labor, and to decisions about sleeping, feeding, and even transporting infants once they're born.

It's not just the difference between a four-figure stroller and a two-figure stroller or between a dainty pram and a wide, thick-wheeled jogging stroller, but the stroller itself as a specific and deliberate mode of transporting a baby that, however grounded in practical concerns, also signals something different from the connotations of baby-wearing. Wearing a baby rather than pushing him in his stroller, or even wearing a baby in an Ergo carrier rather than a sling wrap is commonly assumed to *mean* something, to signal an allegiance to a specific parenting philosophy or set of shared cultural values.

More than two decades after Taylor published her findings, Kim Brooks drew on more contemporary research to make a similar claim, citing Hilary Levey Friedman's description of parents' understandable, if misguided, belief that if they "start soon enough, read the right research, and do the right things, [they] can get the particular end product"—child—they want. Brooks jokes about conducting endless research on "carrying, birthing, and caring for a baby," and bonding with a friend who had a similar due date: "We had lunch whenever we could, bought maternity clothes together, sent each other 'stroller porn,' images of the high-end time-travel-looking contraptions that we couldn't afford but really, really wanted" (43). All of this felt alien to Brooks's sense of self as a woman self-aware enough not to be swayed by transparent marketing campaigns and the notion of cultivating a deliberated parenting philosophy aligned closely with consumption. "I wish I could say I'd never been this person. I wish I could say I found the world of pregnancy vigilance and baby-planning mania pointless and bourgie and gross. . . . I wish I could say that I didn't spend many, many hours of my life deciding which stroller I would buy, or which crib mattress, or which baby monitor, or which baby-wearing sling. . . . I want so badly not to have been the kind of woman who tried to forge an identity— or, help me, God, a . . . brand—out of pregnancy and motherhood, an identity that other women would notice and approve of and admire" (44).

I wish I could say we didn't become a family who owned all five of those strollers (seven if you count the two doll strollers my children owned), and that I too hadn't felt a sense of identity—at once smug and self-conscious— about my dirty running stroller in contrast to the high-end time-travel-looking contraptions I saw in my own days of early parenting. I wish I hadn't internalized the idea that a stroller—or any commodity whose producers stand to benefit from the messaging—was anything other than a potential convenience I was lucky enough to be able to afford.

a "tight" budget out of both necessity and preference, but I don't think anyone could argue broadly for an American culture of frugality regarding spending money—especially when it comes to children and the products for them.

I asked my friend Sarah, a professor of German literature and mother of two young children, for her anecdotal observations about stroller culture both in the United States and in Germany. What were the expectations for children and parents in public spaces, I wanted to know. For example, were German cities, generally speaking, more stroller-friendly, were professional expectations more realistic about the chaos of raising young children, were there structural supports in place in Germany that there are not present in the United States? In response, she wrote: "This is a tricky and somewhat fraught question— it's so easy to fall into the trap of idealizing another country's practices around kids and parenting compared to the US's." In the week we were emailing, Monica Hesse's *Washington Post* op-ed addressing, in part, alarm over the U.S.'s declining birth rate, had been making the rounds in Sarah and my social and professional circles. Though framed by Hesse's personal experience, her essay tackles many parenting practices that either are or feel specific to 21st-century America. At the time of writing, Hesse, was expecting her first child and in her piece she pushes back against the assumptions she's encountered about why she did not have children earlier: that she was immature, lazy, self-focused. Instead, she addresses a long list of reasons that are inherently both personal and cultural that made motherhood feel impossible.

> Pregnancy and childbirth are bloody, messy, flesh-tearing endeavors after which American women are discharged from the hospital with no codified support. No free Finnish baby boxes containing all necessary baby gear. No free British midwives, dropping by your home to check on the mental and physical well-being of the new parents. No free Swedish lactation consultants, no German *hebammen*. No mandated paid maternity leave as exists throughout Europe and in other countries like South Korea, Israel, Mexico, Chile.

It's not just the expectations around pregnancy, delivery, postpartum care or parental leave that contribute to the notion that America is a country that's unfriendly to children and mothers. "I did not have children because America is a difficult place to be a mom," Hesse concludes. "And because every policy-based attempt to change that is met by telling women to buck up, drink a glass of rosé and download the Calm app. Screw that." It's not just *habbemen* (midwives) that make it easy to romanticize the experience of German childrearing. The imaginary childhood of German children that I've dreamed up, the one I was indirectly referring to when I asked Sarah to compare cultures, is one based on a few slice-of-life essays and an assortment of random cultural stereotypes about raising children abroad. In my mind

German childhood is something like an extended, platonic ideal of kindergarten itself—a garden of children learning through Montessori-esque play with sturdy toys made of pale wood.

I've also developed similarly limited and romanticized notions of Scandanavian parenting. A few years ago I read a slew of articles about baby strollers accompanied by images taken outside Swedish daycares on brisk winter afternoons, and skimmed through the early chapters of books like *There's No Such Thing as Bad Weather*, *The Danish Way of Parenting*, and *The Happiest Kids in the World: How Danish Parents Help Their Kids by Doing Less*. Like many of my peers, I've internalized a gauzy narrative that serves mostly as a contrast to the specific cultural demands of raising young children in affluent and upper-middle class America. The romanticized, vague nature of these ideas I had, the inherent superficiality of *notions* or *impressions* as a rule is what makes cultural comparison of any kind difficult and what I think Sarah meant by calling my questions tricky and fraught. But I also understand that the conversations that women are having about the impossibilities and demands of contemporary American motherhood highlight the need to question and challenge some of our own cultural practices by learning about experiences elsewhere.

"I spent a summer in Germany when Elena was 11-13 months old," Sarah wrote after her initial disclaimer, "one month in Freiburg, which is a small city in the southwest, and one in Berlin—and I'd say generally yes, people expect children to be out and about in urban environments and are willing to help with things like subway staircases when elevators are (not infrequently) broken, though you also see a LOT of people with babies and toddlers of varying sizes in wearable carriers, especially in small city centers where navigating a stroller is tricky." In one such instance, Sarah described taking her daughter's stroller on an escalator "because I was in a hurry in an unfamiliar train station and got hissed at the *entire* way up by a (male, of course) German commuter who was mad that he couldn't walk up at his accustomed pace. Which, fair enough—as I said to him, 'I know, I made a mistake'—but he could've said so and then let it go instead of using the entire (interminable, it seemed) escalator ride to lecture me."

Sarah told me that she tends to tell people that overall "Germany is child-friendly but not child-centric; America is child-centric but not child-friendly. My mistake with the escalator was making other people's time revolve around my kid—but when not forced to, other people frequently simply stepped up, without being asked, to help me and my kid navigate urban space." She described "Eltern-Kind Cafes," coffee shops with a playroom for kids and space for adults. "Some are free (except for the coffee), others charge a small entry fee, but the basic *idea* is that parents are human beings who would like to get out of the house sometimes . . . and it would *never* fly in the U.S. because we are a litigious culture instead of an insurance culture (see also: German playgrounds are *amazing* and terrifying!)."

One hot summer day, before I'd realized how inaccessible to strollers the New York City subway system is, I took Thea and Simon on the train from Connecticut to Grand Central by myself. Once we were in midtown, we needed to catch the Times Square Shuttle across town and then the 1-2-3 subway line downtown where I'd picked out a splash pad and ice cream place for us to visit before we'd meet up with Nick when he was done with work for the evening. On earlier family trips to the city, I'd more than once had the exhausting, sweaty experience of telling Thea to grab hold of the stroller's side bar while I hoisted it up, with Simon still in it, and began to struggle with it on the stairs before a stranger wordlessly picked up the stroller's other end and safely shepherded us to the platform below. Every time this happened, I blinked away tears. They were tears of gratitude and relief, but the tears were also because of embarrassment that I'd inconvenienced another passenger, or even many other passengers who had to go around us as we awkwardly descended the stairs. For that reason, before this particular trip on a hot summer day, I'd checked which stations were marked as wheelchair accessible. We hurried across Grand Central to the elevator that was marked on the map which would take us to the subway platform below. I was somewhat surprised to see that there was, in fact, an elevator where the map had promised. When the door opened and I pushed the stroller in with one hand and pulled Thea in after me just as the door began to close, I saw and smelled that the floor was covered in a quarter inch of urine.

"Don't touch anything!" I shouted as we rode. When the doors opened downstairs and I pushed a baby and a preschooler out of the rank enclosure, I felt a new shame—of the ignorance that had led me to instruct my small children to ride down an elevator covered in a stranger's urine.

For the length of our two remaining subway rides, Thea asked me again and again: *who went potty in that elevator?* I offered that I didn't know, then stumbled awkwardly through an attempt to explain that some people don't have access to bathrooms, and then returned to my initial insistence (it *was* true) that I didn't know. Years later, as she and I rode the commuter train to Grand Central with my mom, Thea reported on the incident and asked me again: *who went to the bathroom in that elevator?*

When I asked Wendy about accessibility, she cited Dutch pragmatism as a cultural priority that plays out in the design of public spaces including—but not limited to—the issue of accessibility. "All public places have to have easy access for families including babies and kids in strollers. I have never had an issue to enter any public space; it is a 'have to.' My experience in the US had been very mixed." She cited the NYC subway for example, explaining that "no subway in the Netherlands would be inaccessible for strollers." This is part of a bigger-picture accessibility issue, not just for parents with strollers but for people using wheelchairs or who otherwise might not be able to use the stairs. Just as it extends beyond—and often with greater consequence— the population of parents pushing strollers, the issue of

FIGURE 6 Thea & Simon in in-line stroller in Manhattan.

accessibility extends well beyond elevators in subway systems. "Even in family-friendly places like Fairfield," Wendy said, "[sidewalks], *if* they are there, stop at random spots forcing you to walk on the road with your baby in a stroller. That just does not happen in the Netherlands.

Walkways and bike paths everywhere, no matter how remote the town."

Likewise, the heart of Hesse's *Washington Post* op-ed is larger than the specific engineering of public space, the urban planning that makes a place pedestrian-friendly or not (beyond the question of accessibility of strollers or those using wheelchairs), expectations around meal and snack time, or even legal systems and litigation. Hesse's piece is about the sense of isolation that so many American parents, mothers particularly, feel because of lack of structural support in the form of affordable childcare, paternal leave, and even basic healthcare for parents and young children.

When I was pregnant with Thea, I read *Bringing Up Bébé*, Pamela Druckerman's memoir about raising her children in France. I didn't have a particular interest in French parenting, but the book seemed to be recommended by every list targeted toward women like me. At 32, I wasn't young to be having a baby, but I had only a few friends and peers who'd already done so. It was comforting, though I also see now that it was misguided, to imagine latching on to a catchy, pre-packaged style or philosophy of parenting that might preserve some illusion of originality and refinement that I associate with France and have also never, even pre-motherhood, possessed myself. In France, I learned, all parents had access to free childcare that might include a lunch of poached salmon and soft cheese. In France, I read, children baked treats in the afternoon and waited patiently to eat them at the designated snack hour. In France, mothers went on dates and wore fancy clothes and heels shortly after their babies were born.

The vague sense that it was even more embarrassing to be an American mother than it was to be a mother in general—somehow related to carrying individual bags of goldfish everywhere and relinquishing all personal and professional goals—made the book appealing. *Did you know*, I asked my mom, who surely knew, *that in France, babies eat what the adults eat*? (Actually, I like goldfish crackers, so my American children also eat what I eat.) *In France,* I reported, *when babies cry, the parents wait a minute before rushing in to get them and it makes the kids more patient.*

While reading *Bringing Up Bébé* I attempted the yogurt cake recipe included in the book. Druckerman explains that this cake's measurements are easy enough for a toddler to master and that she sees the act of baking it and waiting for it to cool at the appropriate snack time as exemplars of the maturity, patience and civility made possible by parenting in the French way. While harried American mothers find themselves wearing machine-washable clothes and throwing crumpled individual-portion snack bags to the backseat of a dirty minivan, French mothers seemingly go on living as sophisticated adults, in outfits that require dry cleaning (afterall, there's little chance of food being spilled on it by a patient, polite child who eats his cake at the designated time and with good table manners).

My cake was raw in the middle—inedible. Even as a woman who'd lived on her own for more than a decade, I apparently lacked the kitchen skills of the average French preschool student. As I often had felt as a child when my family lived briefly in French-speaking Switzerland, I was too American, too disorganized, too messy, too impatient and hungry to fit into my vague and simplified version of francophone childhood, let alone capable of sophisticated and dignified francophone motherhood.

Switzerland, though only about the size of Massachusetts, is culturally varied; Paudex, the small village just outside of Lausanne where my family lived, is in the French-speaking region and has more in common with France than with Switzerland's remote alpine villages where a Latin dialect is still spoken, or with the German-speaking area around Zurich or the Italian-speaking ski towns. From my bedroom window, I had a view across Lake Geneva to the snow-capped tops of the French Alps. During the few years we lived there, I had only one friend and I was often doing, wearing, saying, or drawing the wrong thing (not wholly specific to living in Switzerland, but definitely more intense in those years of cultural disconnect). Once the picture of a girl I drew in art class was crossed out with a red pen and the word *faux* (wrong) written next to her plaid skirt. Patterned fabric had not been part of the instructions.

Did I remember, my mom asked in response to my romanticization of French parenting culture, what the public attitude toward children had been in French-speaking Switzerland of the late 1980s? My mom, who, well before we'd known where Paudex was or learned our first sentences of French, had taken me to art museums and given me chores and taught me good table manners and worn dry-clean-only dresses with heels, and introduced me to all kinds of food, who didn't let us whine or demand things and required me to be as patient as my stubborn personality would allow, who read me Arthurian legends and Pernault's fairy tales and all the *Narnia* and *Little House* books, was understandably skeptical of my oversimplified version of another culture's parenting practices as the necessary antidote to the embarrassment of American motherhood.

My mom told me that at one shop she had been asked to leave the pram, and the baby inside it—my two-month-old brother—on the street. Unlike the images of snuggly-bundled Scandinavian babies absorbing their daily allotment of vitamin D and fresh air, or the Danish couple whose Manhattan arrest for leaving their baby napping outside the restaurant where they were having lunch seemed cosmopolitan rather than neglectful, this Swiss boutique's disdain for baby strollers felt more like a disdain for babies, for their crying and their spitting up and the physicality and unpredictability of parenting them. There, signs declaring no children allowed, often in restaurants that welcomed dogs, were common. Even in shops selling children's clothes and toys, children themselves were often *interdit*. I did, once she mentioned this, summon a hazy but tactile memory of standing in the late-80s fluorescent light of a high-end department store, reaching to stroke a soft, pink plush dog before being harshly admonished by the storekeeper and withdrawing my hand with a start.

Because I was young, my most intense memories of the years we spent in Switzerland are mostly personal—about feeling intensely lonely as an American kid speaking badly accented French and writing with over-sized Number Two pencils while my peers were already deftly using fountain pens. Still, many of these memories are magical and dreamy. I remember the sound of the boat to Evian's cheerful *toot* echoing on the lake, the texture of the ice cream cones my dad bought me at the restaurant across the street from his office, the feeling of cobblestone streets under my Mary Janes. Still, despite the delight of those ice cream cones and cobble stones and ancient ruins, the sense I had was that during those years living abroad I was too big (I was a year older than my fellow first graders since I hadn't spoken any French when we arrived) and too unruly. Maybe all this informed the personal appeal of the French baby book.

Perhaps it also explains more generally, the allure of a book promising a less physical, less awkward, less messy version of motherhood, and the publication of hundreds of other France-adjacent books and articles and blog posts promising that—despite the bodily changes and sleep deprivation and the fundamental reorganization of one's life around the survival of another—self-determination, sophistication and order are not at odds with becoming a mother. If the imagined result of French parenting is navy wool-clad children with sophisticated palates patiently waiting until afternoon snack hour to sample the yogurt cake they made, the imagined result of Scandinavian parenting might be healthy children sleeping in minimalist wooden nurseries who play outdoors in all weather (including the weeks of Polar Nights where the sun does not rise inside the arctic circle). Memoirs marketed to American mothers are not limited to one culture and are plentiful enough to comprise their own sub-genre of parenting books.

It is hard to be a parent—everywhere. Children are needy and unpredictable and vulnerable and precious and exhausting, often all at once. It's hard for mothers in France with salmon-serving daycare and it's hard for Dutch mothers pushing sleek and sturdy strollers down smooth sidewalks. Being responsible—emotionally and physically—for the wellbeing of others too small to walk safely on their own or feed themselves is demanding work. Objects, especially objects as prominent, expensive, and visible as a stroller or a carrier, are designed to make some of that work less demanding, and the way those objects are used often suggests something bigger about the way mothers and their children are valued both across and within cultures.

The *New York Times* review of Amber Winick and Michelle Millar Fisher's *Designing Motherhood* ends with an observation about the role of motherhood in American culture. It's not just our contemporary culture: pregnancy and motherhood have long been considered unimportant and the objects themselves point to various ways in which pregnancy and motherhood have been considered taboo or the sole realm of women. Winick and Fisher point out that "[e]ven something as basic as a baby carrier highlights the ways in which our built environment is not meant for parents and children . . . It's a design that, in other ways, helps us with the lack of design in other places, like subway stairs, that are so unfriendly to mothers."

It would be reductive and embarrassing to claim that because a Swiss store once asked my mom to leave a pram outside the Swiss are, as a rule, unwelcoming of mothers and children, or that German mothers are, as a unified entity, more willing to cede independence to their children than their litigation-fearing American counterparts. Sarah was right to remind me of the dangers in romanticizing—or generalizing with a less favorable view—another culture's parenting practices. Still, there certainly seems to be a nexus between the American conflation of consumption with competency and our limited willingness, as a culture, to invest making life more manageable for families with young children. American fascination with simplified versions of other cultural attitudes about parenting are at least in some ways a reaction to what Hesse calls the "unreasonable expectations" of contemporary American motherhood.

4 CARRY THE BABY

Sewell absurdly began his 1923 remarks on the history of prams with the declaration that "the physicians of all countries agree that a woman is not fitted by nature to carry a babe in her arms, on her back, nor on her head or shoulders—these are injurious to both. Hence the need of a miniature carriage." Of course, physicians of all countries do not agree on this—Dr. Sears's support of baby-wearing is a prominent and controversial contemporary example. But, even at the time Sewell addressed his audience, mothers around the world had long been transporting their babies on their backs (or chests) without injuring themselves or their babes.

In *Designing Motherhood*, Winick and Fisher point out that "[d]esigns for baby carrying have precedents in every corner of the globe, including in the tied textiles of the African continent, Plains Indian cradleboards, and in parts of Asia, special cold-weather carrier covers embroidered with motifs that are meant to assure a child's good fortune" (page 278). Photographs in the book show babies in soft slings, shawls

FIGURE 7 Zapatista Army mothers with baby carriers.

and structured carriers and in places ranging from Thailand, to the Civil Rights march from Selma to Montgomery, to La Gamucha, Mexico where mothers in the Zapatista Army of National Liberation pose for the camera with their infants across their chests, one nursing from a sling.

In 2004, Nairobi store owner Irene Wambui told *The Guardian* that she couldn't imagine why anyone would buy a baby stroller, calling them "a cold cage filled with useless rattles, cup holders and mirrored headlights." She likened children in strollers to animals being "pushed around town like some kind of pet." In the middle-class shopping district where Wambui's shop is located, even among mothers working outside the home, strollers had not been widely adopted. This was, Emily Wax writes, because "[t]he introduction of strollers and baby carriages, both known here by the British word 'pram,' horrifies traditionalists, even someone such as Wambui, who sells them. The stroller is appearing in major cities around Africa, but so far has not been a hit."

Wambui explained: "In Africa we just carry our children or let them roam. They can't sit like lumps." As I read the word "lumps," I thought guiltily of Simon's long legs hanging nearly to the ground as I pushed him to and from preschool, recalling the vague embarrassment I often felt over having him in a stroller at his size and age, and the competing, somewhat defensive sense that while the school commute was a pleasant mile for an me, as an adult, to stroll, it was a long, slow, patience-trying journey with a four-year old who was also on foot. And anyway—it would have been more absurd for me to carry him to or from school (though on occasion when we forewent the stroller, I allowed him to ride on my shoulders, giggling and pulling at my hair for blocks at a time, which was exhausting and also made me feel superhuman). If I hadn't used the stroller, most likely he'd have been strapped into his car seat to drive three minutes down the road and then spend five minutes looking for parking. Still, the lump simile hit close to home, particularly later in the article when Wax cited concern from American pediatricians over the relationship between late stroller use and childhood obesity.

"Besides," Wambui explained "[Nairobi] roads aren't even good enough for these devices. If everyone had a pram it would cause jam-ups in traffic. Then we would be bad to our children and bad to our roads." The cost also made them prohibitive; even inexpensive strollers, like the one Wambui sold in her shop for about $60, would have accounted for nearly half a typical mother's monthly wages. One of Wambui's customers described prams as "pricey," and another, a government secretary who stopped in for baby bottles, called them "oppressive."

Frank Njenga, a child psychiatrist based in Nairobi, told Wax that "[the] pram is the ultimate in pushing the baby away from you . . . The baby on the back is actually following the mother in warmth and comfort. The baby feels safer, and safer people are happier." Njenga's condemnation brought to mind similar-stroller opposition from a very different context. I thought of L.N., the fictional Prius-driving University of Wisconsin professor from Sam Mendes's 2009 film *Away We Go*. In response to receiving a stroller as a gift, L.N. (pronounced "Ellen") begins to scream with revulsion: "I love my children! Why would I push them away from me?" The line, in context, works as a punchline that reveals the absurdity of L.N.'s smug parenting philosophies, but it also evokes Dr. Sears's attachment parenting advice and the persistent, if not pervasive, notion that there's something cold and aloof about putting a baby in a stroller.

When I've heard impassioned stroller-opposition in my own real life, it has often been from women very much like L.N.: affluent, well-educated, white, American, vaguely progressive proponents of attachment parenting (a philosophy they often reference by that specific term). L.N. is fervently pro-family bed. "Are you planning on hiding your lovemaking from your kids?" she demands of Burt and Veronica, her stroller-gifting guests. She follows up by asking if they "know what it does to a child to have their parents' expression of love kept a secret?" Most viewers, like me, will side with Burt and Verona who exchange open looks of horror as L.N. continues, explaining that she and her husband live in what they call "a continuum home" where they fervently oppose the three Ss: separation, sugar, and strollers. If this movie were made in 2021, it might reference the four Ss and include screens.

FIGURE 8 Still from *Away We Go* with stroller in foreground.

L.N., played by Maggie Gyllenhaal, is a type, and it was something of a personal relief to laugh at her. I never planned to ban sugar from the house, share a giant, room-sized mattress with my nuclear family or to nurse my children into early elementary school, the way she does, but I had thought breastfeeding would be easier than it was, and that I'd do it longer than I did. I harbored golden-hued fantasies of stirring vegetarian risotto with a baby cooing or lightly snoring in a ring sling while a toddler played quietly with wooden educational toys. Instead, when Thea only weighed ten pounds at four months, I'd been sent home from the pediatrician's office with a free sample of formula that I gave to her in the backseat of my Prius while Nick went into Stop and Shop to buy several more cases of Similac. I was so fervently anti-screens that I (psychotically) demanded family members turn off sports games that were playing in the room where my kids were playing until Simon was two. But then Thea couldn't join in the class game of *Frozen* on the preschool playground because she didn't know what it was, and so we let her watch that and she did not become any less curious or active or thoughtful than she had been before. In the end, my children—who eat desert daily and once drank formula and rode in strollers and have slept in their own beds since they were just a few weeks old—now enjoy some screen time while I make dinner (which is never, it should go without saying, vegetarian risotto).

The tension between the mother who nurtures—nuzzling her children in a literal and figurative nest of maternal patience—and the mother who does not—walking briskly down the street while pushing them away from her—comes up over and over again across centuries of art portraying mothers and their children. In its early-21st-century iteration, things like breastfeeding (especially older babies or toddlers), baby-wearing, technology-using, and working outside the home are collective, cultural shorthands for identifying which side of the nurturing divide a mother falls on. L.N. works, but at The University of Wisconsin-Madison, a famously liberal university, in the humanities, and with an unexplained flexibility that allows for both of her children to be in her tapestry-decorated office, tandem nursing when Verona and Burt first meet her. L.N. has made at least one enemy on campus because of her parenting practices: once, without permission, she nursed a colleague's child while she was helping his mother by babysitting him.

Throughout the film, Verona and Burt meet other parents who also fill a specific cultural niche: there are the heavy drinking, cursing parents who disparage their children openly when they are in earshot and make a lot of jokes about the effect of lactation on breast firmness and shape. There are the white Canadian parents who have struggled to get pregnant and adopted five nonwhite children, and there is the newly single father who is trying desperately to protect his daughter from the full weight of her mother's abandonment. But, it is insufferable L.N. who so clearly illustrates the way mothers often find themselves trapped between the archetype of the too-aloof mother (like Betty Draper with her enormous and rigid tank-like pram) on one hand, and the L.N. on the other.

In the dorm I lived in during my freshman year of college, a young married couple—graduate students, I think—had been assigned to live there and generally keep an eye on us. Once a month they'd invite residents of the dorm (which our university called a "house") to their two-dorm-room-sized apartment, and we'd play a get-to-know-you game over snacks. The events weren't mandatory and even as a very sincere person, I found them overly earnest, and so avoided them after the first time I attended. Part of what contributed to this feeling of earnestness and sincerity was the married couple themselves. They must have been in their mid-twenties, though they seemed so much older to me then, the husband with a square jaw and the woman with a body that was not overweight exactly but changed in the particular way of one that has borne children. She often wore their youngest child in a sling carrier—I think there were three blonde little boys, but I somewhat deliberately, in an attempt to show my disinterest in children and marriage and general domesticity, found them indistinct. I remember laughing with my friends at their whole affect. The sling, the fact that they'd taught their children sign language, not because of hearing loss, but because it would allow the babies to communicate before they might be developmentally or physiologically able to do so vocally.

Even though the practice of baby-wearing was not new in 2000, when my dorm-mates and I thought a baby in a sling was noteworthy enough to be a distinguishing familial characteristic, it was uncommon in worlds I'd inhabited. My mom had pushed my brother in a pram and I'd seen participants in local road races pushing jogging strollers, but while it had become increasingly common in the United States in the second half of the twentieth century, I can't remember ever seen anyone wearing a baby in a sling or a carrier.

Aradia Wyndham, drawing on her training as an anthropologist, writes about the history of pregnancy and infant care for her blog *The Baby Historian*. She argues that the post-Second World War baby boom marked a change— or at least the beginning of a change—in attitudes about baby-wearing in the United States. Wyndham's research chronicles artistic representation of baby-carrying from the walls of a 3,500 year old Egyptian tomb, to Middle Ages (including depictions of Christ being carried by St. Christopher in a sling), to Indian statues of Rani Lakshmibai fighting on horseback while wearing a baby on her back, to modern American references in the 1951 Spencer Tracy film *Daddy's Little Dividend* and Lorraine Hainsbury's *A Raisin in the Sun* where baby-wearing serves as shorthand for performing demanding labor while also caring for a child. "The use of infant carriers wasn't a novel concept in North America in the 20th century," she explains "but it [has] had a stigma of poverty or transience attached . . . in the West since the Middle Ages."

As baby-wearing has become more common and more popular in the United States there has predictably been some pushback about the extent to which Western women adopting the practice amounts to cultural appropriation. Wyndham's scholarship presents a convincing argument that baby-wearing has long been a part of Western culture even if it came to be associated with working class and poor mothers as stroller use became more widespread. I rarely used my baby carrier the way I'd imagined I would. The one time I cooked dinner wearing Simon while Thea played, it was so noteworthy I took a triumphant whole-family selfie. I used the carrier on a handful of occasions: hikes, apple-picking expeditions, and trips to the city when either Thea or Simon was still less than six months old, when moving

FIGURE 9 Morgan family with baby Simon in sling.

through these spaces of uneven terrain or crowded stairs with my hands free and a curled infant nestled on my front was easier, and yes, sweeter, than snapping and unsnapping five-point harnesses.

Although at 18, I found the cultural shorthand that American women wearing their babies signified too sincere and earnest, by the time I sat across from Ann at dinner, I felt an increasing desire for the sincere and earnest. In my books about how French mothers raise children or the secret to Norwegian children's happiness or books about baby-led weaning, I was looking for a way to reconcile the person who'd rolled her eyes—both with Ann at my peers' baby showers, and at the graduate students trying to raise a family in a college dorm—with the person who wanted to have children in large part because she wanted to walk through a beautiful and frightening world while holding them close.

But in practice, I found the wrap difficult to tie so that it felt truly secure, and no matter how hard I tried, my body did not make enough milk to feed Thea, and I was never organized or patient enough to make my own baby food, and so we bought strollers and formula and pouches of pureed baby food that surely contained sugar and weren't always organic.

When I first started giving Thea formula, I worried about running out of it, about not having access to water to mix with the powder, about forgetting, losing, or somehow being unable to use baby bottles. I hated the idea that there was something she needed, not just for comfort or for maximal stimulation, but for survival that I might not be able to provide her. At the height of American media coverage of the Syrian refugee crisis, I learned of an organization collecting gently used baby carriers for mothers traveling on foot, and I sent mine away. For days after I'd mailed it off, I imagined it making its way to eastern Europe while I read to my children at bedtime, and I hoped soon it would be holding a baby, making another mother's harrowing journey even just the tiniest bit easier.

5 THE PRAM IN THE HALL

Cyril Connolly: There is no more sombre enemy of good art than the pram in the hallway.

Shane Jones: The pram in the hall was no somber enemy—rather, because I was baggy-eyed, vein-drenched in coffee, and blindly stepping into the new world of fatherhood, producing work had never felt more important to me.

Steven Wingate: So when I hear see Cyril Connolly say that having kids . . . is the enemy of good art, please pardon me for getting apoplectic. For me, not having kids turned out to be the enemy of good art. Becoming a father meant finally being forced by circumstance to claim a plot of metaphorical land where I had to dig my own ditches, cut my own trees, and build my own literary home. No crowds or cliques would make a difference. There was nothing left but me and the words that poured out of my fingers. . . . And oh yeah—the pram in the hallway that finally gave my life a meaning beyond my own wants.

Stephanie Merritt: For about the first decade of my son's life I thought Cyril Connolly had it bang to rights. This despite the fact that, of the eight books I've written, seven were produced while also trying to be a mother. I say "trying" because there is always this sense that you are scrambling to catch up, never feeling on top of things, short-changing your work and your child. That's a feeling common to most working mothers, I think, whatever their profession, but creative work makes particular demands that are, in my experience, not easy to reconcile with parenthood. Most obviously, creating art demands the best of your energy and attention. So do children. People think being a writer must be an ideal job to fit around raising a child because it's so flexible, but those people have usually not written novels. When you're immersed in creating an imaginary world, you have to live inside it, and that requires time and solitude—both of which are in short supply for mothers. It's true that being a parent opens up a range of emotional experience that can be invaluable for novelists, dramatists or songwriters, but, as with any demanding job, you can only really do it if you have someone else on hand to do all the boring, routine, nuts-and-bolts parts of looking after children.

Shane Jones: I was creatively explosive, if a little loose and wild. I can't remember showering or looking in the mirror for weeks. Given the sudden constrains on my time, the pockets in which I could work were like mines where I hacked away with a speed I've never experienced before, discovering and polishing work. . . . I do realize that I'm writing this from a place of privilege, as a white, educated male with a relaxed day job that allows me the brain space for ideas such as this very piece. Trying to imagine myself as a full-time, stay-at-home mother, trying to work on a novel with an infant attached to my breast, sends a chill through me. It would be much harder to get work done .My wife, Melanie, is our son's primary caregiver, a full-time student, and works part-time as a massage therapist. Where I can come to the office and grab a cup of coffee, she has little to no time with her own thoughts.

Stephanie Merritt: I certainly agree that the pressures do concentrate the mind; I am more driven and waste far less time than I used to. I wrote my second novel while on maternity leave in a kind of frenzy, at night, in the gaps while my son slept. But I wouldn't recommend that way of working to anyone, even though there are famous examples of people who have made it work. If you're going to make good art, the creative process requires space to daydream, to immerse yourself in the project, and, above all, to risk failure.

Amanda Parrish Morgan: In some ways, though, I've found that parenthood *is* conducive to a certain kind of immersion—at least in the sense of dreaming. As I walked through our neighborhood, I noticed things about the people, the houses, the landscape that I never had before. On long car rides, while the soundtrack to *Frozen* played, my mind wandered in a way it doesn't when I'm listening to *All*

Things Considered or an audiobook at 1.25 speed—maybe in a way that was subconsciously incorporated the magic of children's stories and children's questions.

Frank Cottrell Boyce: My children have been a crucial part of my work in ways that I find hard to account for or anticipate. If I need to go on a research trip for a book or a film, we'll usually go as a family, and I find that—apart from the fact that it's useful to have extra eyes and ears—people and places tend to open up to you more.

Stephanie Merritt: Perhaps Connolly was touching on a larger point: namely that, when you become a parent, your art is no longer the single biggest priority in your life, to which you dedicate all your time and energy, and that can feel like a compromise at first.

Amanda Parrish Morgan: Pushing our stroller slowed me down in a way that let me see and think in ways I hadn't before. And often, at the end of those walks or runs with my children I'd park the stroller in the grass or in the hall and take out my laptop and write as fast as I could, even if my idea wasn't perfect, while one of my children snored softly, napping safe and peaceful at my side. It was the way I could be the primary caregiver for our children and get time with my own thoughts.

6 PRAMS OF GOOD AND EVIL

My first ideal of motherhood, before *Bringing Up Bébé* or the phrase "attachment parenting" or the ascription of maternal devotion to months of breastfeeding completed, came from the framed print of Mary Cassatt's *Mother and Child on a Green Background* hanging in my childhood bedroom. I'd chosen the print from the Musee D'Orsay when my mom and I visited just before my brother was born. I was seven years old and already beginning to sense, especially with the knowledge that there would soon be an infant in the house, that my own childhood was quickly moving behind me. I was also beginning to see babies and sponge baths and prams as something sweet and gentle that I wanted to miss, wanted to feel a little sentimental about.

In *Mother and Child on a Green Background*, a young Victorian mother, her brown hair in a neat but soft bun, nuzzles against the cheek of her baby, who is facing forward, dressed in a white nightgown and sucking on a plump hand. As in many of Cassatt's paintings, there is something preternaturally kind about the mother and something cherubic but not cloying about the baby. Even in years of adolescent grouchiness, of lonely young-adulthood, I kept the print (though in my closet instead of on the wall), and now it hangs in the bedroom that was first Thea's and then Simon's.

Trying to ascribe value to the work that mothering requires can sometimes rely on caricaturizing or even mocking children—the sometimes-mundane nature of feeding, cleaning and dressing of young babies, the inane requirements of preschool social events, the potential to lose sight of oneself in the demands of parenting. At the same time, understanding the demands of motherhood also requires acknowledgement of those same children's vulnerability, openness, wonder, and the resulting threat, as a parent, of becoming overwhelmed. And yet, a narrative that positions motherhood as an ordained social, moral or even religious Good, not just for children but for the women who become their mothers, evokes Victorian-era notions of the Cult of Domesticity and 21st-century forays into biological essentialism. The truth of what makes both mothering and having been mothered valuable to me contains the mundane and inane, the acknowledgement of vulnerability, and, tricky as it can be to articulate, the moral responsibility that comes with raising children carefully.

At some point as an adult, I learned that many people find Cassatt too sentimental. I understand this perspective, but do not share it. The gentleness of her mothers, the bare baby bottoms, the mix of longing and fulfillment in both sets of eyes, the wooded paths and row boats and sitting rooms and park benches all evoke a personal confidence in the purity and endurance of maternal love. The conflation of motherhood with purity has the potential to be both sentimental and dangerous, but I think Cassatt's paintings are neither.

I love Mary Cassatt's paintings because they remind me of how it feels to have been raised by my loving, generous, gentle, thoughtful mom. Cassatt's work also evokes the physicality—the round cheeks, the bathtubs, the holding close—of the early years I spent with my own children. What I feel about my children *is* sentimental. The desire I have to hold them tight and clean and safe is so all-consuming that it exists on both literal and abstract levels at the same time. I prepare meals, put on sunscreen, require bike helmets, clip car seats and stroller buckles; and even now that they are not plump, cherubic babies, but long-limbed children, I feel an intense mix of relief and purpose and satisfaction when, wet-haired and freshly clean from the tub after a long day playing in the woods, they fall asleep against me while I read aloud from a book about the magic of fairies or wizards or talking foxes.

In "Mary Cassatt: Modern Woman or the Cult of True Womanhood," Norma Broude explains the lens through which Cassatt, a woman who never had children and achieved a great deal professionally and publicly, came to be championed by a certain subset of conservative Victorian women:

FIGURE 10 Cassatt's *The Nurse*.

"Cassatt's images of happy and fulfilled mothers, surrounded by children who are the personification of goodness and innocence, these pictures that deify motherhood and its joys, were painted in an era of great, even hysterical public concern over declining birthrates in France," a concern loudly echoed in contemporary American conversation. Victorian attitudes toward women's worth were often narrowly constrained by arguments about the morality of motherhood—women deserved respect because motherhood was profound moral and ethical work—and the neat Victorian sorting of men and women through "the concept of 'equality in difference,'" a philosophy that "advocated the sexual division of labor in society and the family" (Broude). Certainly, motherhood ought to be valued, including for the profound ethical and moral work that it involves. But that Victorian tendency to define women's value by motherhood alone complicated both Cassatt's work and its reception: if a woman's value is defined by her work as a mother, what about depictions of motherhood made by a woman who is not herself a mother?

In so many of the fairy tales or classic children's novels I read to Thea and Simon, loving mothers, women who are warm and soft, are juxtaposed with women who are cold and distant. Sometimes these women are stepmothers or witches or begrudging caretakers of orphans. When my children spend hours in the worlds of their shared imagination, the villains of worlds are mashups of *A Little Princess*'s Miss Minchin and *The Lion, the Witch and the Wardrobe*'s Jadis, and Rapunzel's kidnapping witch-mother from the Disney movie. I like to tell myself that perhaps in these imaginary scenarios, Mary Cassatt mothers, who I hope I might resemble on my best days, are just out of scene waiting to draw them a bath. The good mother archetype to counter the bad. After all, many of the images of Victorian motherhood, like the ornate, expensive pram as prized consumer object that's owned by the elite but used primarily by the servant class, are directly in conversation with archetypes of mothers and caregivers.

In Irish writer Roddy Doyle's short story "The Pram," Alina, a Polish nanny—maybe a modern update to Cassatt's nurse?—with an unnerving mix of sympathetic back-story and murderous delusions, spends her initial days with a wealthy Dublin family pushing their youngest child on long morning walks in an old-fashioned pram. Alina's employer, a withholding, controlling and cruel woman, has told her older daughters that the baby's pram is haunted. Alina loathes these spoiled and cruel older children but cares tenderly for the baby, and with him she walks a path along the water where she meets a lover, an act for which she is eventually humiliated.

Doyle's story, written in 2005, reads as contemporary, and as a result, the pram feels deliberately anachronistic. Alina observes that she hasn't seen anything like it in years, and that it reminds her of the perambulator her grandmother used to use. At the same time, the pram is an important piece of equipment for Alina's employer, a cellphone-attached woman with a high-status career who, even to her children, goes only by her last name (O'Reilly)—seemingly even more important than the baby inside. "Don't scrape the sides," she tells Alina, "it is very valuable." When Alina asks if the pram is a family heirloom, O'Reilly replies "No . . . we bought it . . . just be careful with it." By contrast to the cumbersome, old-fashioned pram, the other women Alina passes on her daily walks "pushed modern, lighter baby-conveyances, four wheeled and three. Alina envied them. The pram felt heavy and the wind from the sea constantly bashed against its hood."

Many Victorian images of babies in prams—black and white stiff-bodied photographs, or Mary Cassatt's *The*

Nurse: Child in a Garden, for example—show not a mother, but a paid caretaker with the child. It's as though, as Irene Wembui implied, the rigid sides of the pram, the literal arm's length from the caregiver pushing it, are understood to signal an emotional rigidity and distance as well. In Doyle's story, the mother's focus on the pram's monetary value and resulting eagerness to make the baby's mode of transport into something frightening in order to preserve it illustrates her coldness. But even Alina, who is warmer in her engagement with the baby, uses the pram as a means of distancing herself from him. When Alina meets her lover on her daily walks with the pram, the baby lies off to the side while the couple kiss. "[The baby] smiled; he bucked. He started to cry. The pram rocked on its springs" (Doyle 158).

Writing for the *Canadian Journal of Irish Studies*, Molly E. Ferguson sees *The Deportees*, the collection in which "The Pram" appears, as centrally concerned with the ways Ireland was renegotiating its relationship with emigration in the early years of the 21st-century. Through this lens, the relationship between Alina and her abusive employer feels emblematic of a larger reckoning with class and power. When Alina begins to expand the story O'Reilly has been telling about the pram being haunted into a ghost story to scare the entitled older daughters, she does so out of malice. Alina hates them and wishes to kill them, though "she would not in actuality, kill the girls. She could not do such a thing . . . she would however frighten them" (160).

Alina's haunted pram story involves woodcutters, a witch in a dark forest who kidnaps all the babies in town, taking them away in a rusty old pram in order to steal their skin. The tale becomes so vivid that both the older girls and Alina herself begin to believe it. At "The Pram's" conclusion, Alina murders her employer in the midst of a psychotic break and then walks the pram into the sea where, through the luck of mucky low-tide, the wheels are stuck and the baby is rescued before he is carried away by the water. The story ends with an image of the empty pram being swallowed by the Irish sea: "He lay on [a quilt] on top of the mud. The tide was out but coming back. The water was starting to fill and swallow the quilt. They lifted the baby and the struggling woman onto the bridge. They left the pram in the rising water" (178).

The police find only one baby, we learn, in that expensive, valuable pram, despite the stories Alina had begun to believe about it being haunted by many. But, even if it's not haunted in the sense Alina's story suggests, the pram with its Victorian aesthetic and impracticality and status signaling does come to seem like a dangerous relic, the smashing together of things that are out of synch: traditional and quickly changing Ireland, a pram and a cell phone, the presence and rigidity of the big, unwieldy pram alongside the softness of a tiny infant, an aloof and cold mother, a neglectful and violent caregiver, safety and danger, infancy and mortality.

When I asked my friend Sarah about Germany's child-friendliness, in addition to her insights about infrastructure and accessibility in public places, she pointed out something else—it can be difficult to distinguish child-friendliness from traditional notions that women and men ought to occupy separate spheres:

> One other thing that seems important to mention is that *some* of [Germany's] child-friendliness, especially in less urban environments/more conservative areas . . . is also coupled with old-fashioned sexism—when I saw your email, one of the first words that popped into my head was "*Rabenmutter*," which means raven mother and is an insult still used for women who work and thus "let their children be raised by someone else." Schools sometimes still have non-standard hours (one day longer than another, home for lunch, whatever), and one of the reasons Germany adopted family-friendly *policies* was that women were looking at the obstacles and choosing not to have children, so the birth rate fell.

Revering motherhood, even lauding the important work of motherhood, comes close to revering women specifically and only *for* motherhood and is both limited and limiting. In this way, the notion of a haunted pram or the threat of a baby separated (pushed away in L.N.'s words) from its mother being vulnerable to exploitation or harm by encroaching mobs, witches, psychotic nannies, endangered by their *rabenmutters* is tapping into that same insistence on tying women's worth to their status as mothers—the insistence that women are either deserving of respect only *in spite* of being mothers or only *because* of being mothers.

In my quest to find photographs and paintings of old-fashioned perambulators and baby carriages, I came across a still from the 1925 movie *The Battleship Potemkin*. The image shows a crying baby in a pram, headed down stone steps strewn with dead and wounded bodies. I'd not yet seen the film, but the image was viscerally familiar.

The Battleship Potemkin is a 1925 Soviet silent film about a mutiny aboard a Russian ship and the resulting confrontation between supporters of the revolution and the military on the streets of Odessa. In the film's fourth act, called "The Odessa Steps," unarmed civilians are shot—elderly men and women,

FIGURE 11 Still of pram on stairs from *Battleship Potemkin*.

a man without use of his legs, a child who is trampled as he lies bleeding, and a mother who collapses against her baby's pram, sending it down the long, cement steps to certain death. Writing for *Salon*, Andrew O'Hehir argues that the scene on the steps has been profoundly influential not just because "the terrifying massacre staged by Eisenstein on the seafront steps of Odessa has been repurposed any number of times, from Brian De Palma's 'The Untouchables' to George Lucas' 'Star Wars Episode III: Revenge of the Sith' to 'Naked Gun 33 1/3,' but . . . [because] 'Potemkin' pioneered what became a staple Hollywood genre, the heavily fictionalized, inspirational retelling of historical events, built around easily recognizable archetypes of good and evil."

When we moved to Switzerland I was in the first grade. I knew no one and no French and so I spent a lot of time at home alone reading. I especially liked Roald Dahl's books in those years, I think in part because of the very clear—cartoonish, even—division between good and evil characters. Some of the adults in my world were, like so many of Dahl's adults, controlling and vindictive. My parents were loving and patient and did everything they could to make living in a foreign country a cosmopolitan, delicious, beautiful adventure, but the nuns at my Swiss school might as well have been caricatures of both Swiss and Catholic school stereotypes of cold, rigid discipline. I sat quietly in the back row where I'd been assigned due to my dictation and penmanship scores being among the lowest in the class, I was spared the corporal punishment some of the other students received (ruler slaps, heads held under cold water—something I now find it almost impossible to believe actually happened). The combination of feeling powerless and lonely and odd and misunderstood and indignant about the cruelty of adults made scenes like the one in which Matilda gets revenge on her cruel teacher satisfying, or the possibility of child-killing witches roaming barely-disguised among us resonant.

The film version of Dahl's *The Witches* came out in 1990. No matter how many times I watched it, a scene that I had somehow barely registered when I read the book always made my stomach drop. Angelica Houston as the Grand High Witch pushes a baby pram, with the baby inside, off a cliff. Perhaps it was because by then, I had a baby brother and my mom had often pushed him in an old-fashioned pram, our cocker spaniel's leash looped around the handle, as we walked into town, and because I knew how delicate a baby was, how soft its head, how much care was required to keep one safe.

When I watched the scene recently, I did so on mute because Simon was in the other room and I couldn't bear for him to hear the baby screaming while Luke, the story's hero, chases after the pram. Even without the sound on, all the hair on my arms stood up and, without realizing it, I brought my hand over my mouth in horror. The baby cries, the witches—holding their noses because children smell like feces to them—laugh and cheer with glee, and Luke and the baby's mother chase frantically after the pram until Luke grabs its handle at the very last second. The fear evoked in the scene

FIGURE 12 Still from *The Witches* with pram on cliff.

is so primal—it's impossible not to imagine the baby's head being dashed on the rocks below, while its mother watches helpless to save her child.

When I told Nick about *Battleship Potemkin*'s pram scene as the inspiration for a variety of similar scenes made in homage or parody, he asked me if I remembered the pram scene from *Ghostbusters II*. Susan Sarandon, balancing two brown paper bags of groceries and a stately pram down a Manhattan sidewalk, pauses to talk to a passerby. While she's stopped, the pram begins to roll away, and then, as if steered by a deliberate and invisible maniac, weaves in and out of people and traffic before she's able to grab it. The baby's face is so sweet and full of frightened wonder that it made the entire movie unwatchable to me as a kid. Had I not left the room crying as a child, I would have seen that it also sets up the imperative for the Ghostbusters to succeed in the context of real threat (even if it is campily-rendered) to innocent bystanders.

In *Ghostbusters II, The Witches, Battleship Potemkin* and "The Pram," babies and their prams function as archetypes of innocence. That it's the pram, rather than a baby itself, thrown down cliffs and steps feels significant beyond the dramatic tension brought by the (however small) possibility of the child's survival. It is ironic that the babies' vulnerability comes from the very thing intended to keep them safe. It's as though the protection, structural stability, and high-class status a pram signals is not only incapable of truly protecting the infant inside, but the wheels, the rigid sides, the separation from the mother is a primary and potentially even insurmountable risk. The pram as a central object in these scenes feels Victorian not just because the pram itself *looks* Victorian but because its rigid fussiness seems to distill something about the Cult of Domesticity and idealized notions of motherhood and femininity that defined that era just as the travel-system and carbon-fiber running stroller might reveal something about our own.

Even L.N.'s very 21st-century rant about the stroller's symbolic meaning gets at the same questions Broude is asking about Mary Cassatt's depictions of motherhood and caregiving. The implication is that the wheels, the very convenience of pushing a baby through the city streets, is itself a risk. And it is—though not necessarily a greater risk than a child breaking free from his mother and darting into traffic or being left home alone, as was the alternative in the case of one mother whose need for a stroller in a 1910 *New York Times* classified ad.

How dangerous are strollers in real life? How likely is it for a child to be fatally injured while riding in one? I held my breath while I read the Consumer Product Safety Commission (CPCS) statistics on stroller deaths. It made no difference that the report, "Injuries Associated with Strollers," stated multiple times that there had been only 20 stroller-related deaths in the years between 1990 and 1999; with each anecdotal explanation of a stroller dropped while being carried on the stairs or a baby becoming entangled in unclipped harness straps, I ran back through an instance when I had put Thea or Simon in a similar situation. By the time I had read halfway through the agency's report, my head throbbed from grinding my teeth. *Twenty deaths in nine years is vanishingly small*, I told myself. *My children are mostly out of strollers. Almost all of those babies were sleeping, were under six months, surely strollers are safer now, the regulations about straps more strict—surely this could not happen outside the screen or the page or the newspaper and in my own goldfish-crumb encrusted, non-archetypal life.* Through these mental acrobatics, I realized that even as a little girl, I'd sensed the possibility of loss in Cassatt's paintings. In fact, the awareness is what had always kept the tenderness of those paintings from seeming sentimental. I'd also understood the danger of those careening prams to be much more real, to be pointing toward something universal and visceral, rather than a convenient trope of fantasy or science fiction.

There was no way to ask the teacher a private question, no access to a quick last-minute bathroom stop, and it was difficult to prevent little siblings from toddling and climbing up and down the cramped staircase. I dreaded the process of entering school and tried to thread the needle between arriving late enough that we wouldn't have to wait long but not so late that Thea would have to go in through the front door, a process that was not really a big deal logistically but caused her a great deal of embarrassment.

One morning, I'd run as fast as I could with the double running stroller, sprinted really, not out of a desire to log more intense training, but because we were cutting it a little close. When we got in line, there were only two children left waiting in front of Thea. I was sweating and frazzled. I put the stroller's brake down and with Simon still strapped in and parked at the end of the blacktop where he could watch a class of three-year-olds play on the tire swing. Thea had to go to the bathroom, or maybe she had to ask her teacher a question—for some reason, it took longer than it might ordinarily have to wait in line while three children said good morning and then walked into a church basement. When I came back up the half-flight of stairs, maybe a minute or two later, there was a commotion. Someone was shouting from inside the fence by the tire swing: *whose baby is this?*

I thought there had been a horrible accident—something like what I'd gritted my teeth and held my breath against in the stroller safety report. Simon had somehow tipped the stroller over? He'd tried to climb out and gotten stuck? But there it was sitting upright, he was constrained by the five-point harness. I thought then that maybe he was screaming? But I heard no toddler screaming, only adult shouting. Perhaps he was sick, he'd vomited, he'd broken a rule, somehow, from inside his stroller seat. I ran toward him. The father of a student in Thea's class looked at me kindly, which I later realized was because he already knew what I was going to hear and he wanted me to know he thought I'd done nothing wrong.

There were three teachers standing near Simon's stroller, and I was told the director was on her way. "Is this your baby?" someone asked.

"Yes," I said. Was he okay? What happened?

"He's fine. He's happy." She must have seen my panic. By this point, the sympathetic-look-giving dad had already turned and walked to his car but a few mothers remained, watching mid-chat, workout clothes already on in anticipation of the gym, coffee cups in hand. "But," she continued, "he could have been kidnapped."

I must have looked taken-aback, because she said, "I know Fairfield feels like a safe town, but you never know."

You never do know. But kidnappings—like stroller deaths—are exceedingly rare. Obviously any kidnapping of any child is horrible, but that particular horrible situation evoked at preschool drop-off is less likely than any number of risks most of us take day in and day out. And yet, "stereotypical kidnappings," the Department of Justice's term for stranger abductions, loom large in our collective imagination.

I'm not sure if I ever actually *saw* a missing child's photograph on a milk carton, but the notion of entire ranks of children who were so hopelessly lost that the dairy industry was the last great hope in finding them was a staple of middle-grade mysteries and my most vivid anxieties. The myth of stranger abductions fueled many of my own childhood afternoons sprinting through the woods, terrified by the sighting of an unmarked white van. Even all these years later a memory of that van is somewhere in the back of my mind whenever I'm scanning the playground to make sure I have eyes on my kids. But, at the preschool, where Simon was surrounded by teachers and parents he and I both knew, on a blacktop inaccessible to cars off of a road with no available parking and sitting there without me for just a few moments, I had not even factored the possibility of kidnapping into my decision to leave him in the stroller. I had considered the judgement from other adults. But I'd decided no matter what they might think that he'd be both more content and safer. Happily watching older kids play, I figured, was better than trying to toddle up and down basement stairs between and among small children, their over-sized school bags and their harried parents.

I didn't say any of this to the frantic adults. I'd already done all the protesting and defending myself that I felt I had a right to under the circumstances. Instead, I kissed Simon's head over and over again, squeezed his little hand, and walked home slowly. While I pushed the stroller down the blocks we traveled several times a day, I held tight to his

FIGURE 13 Thea and Simon in tandem stroller.

hand through an opening in the stroller canopy. I thought about how if something *had* happened to him, some of these people might have thought that I deserved the unbearable sorrow and guilt that would follow. I thought that maybe some of those onlookers thought I didn't love Simon enough, that somehow against the very reality of parenthood, I was not living my life with the visceral knowledge that his tiny, delicate life was in my guardianship. Of course, I know this so well that even thinking it, let alone writing it, feels dangerous; but, to an outside observer it might appear that I did not yet know deep down that the gift of Simon in our lives could be cut short through any number of horrible accidents or illnesses or violence at any time. I said to him what I always say to my children when I've been too quick to anger or they have a fever or there is a wrong in the world that I have caused and cannot fix: *I love you so much*, like an incantation that might protect us both.

A similar event was the impetus for Kim Brooks's *Small Animals,* an exploration of, as her subtitle puts it, "parenthood in the age of fear." In Brooks's case, a stranger watched as, in a hurry before a flight from her parents' house in Virginia back home to Chicago, she allowed her four-year-old son to stay in the car on a cool morning while she quickly went into Target to purchase a pair of headphones. The stranger called the police and showed them a video he or she had taken of the incident. By the time the police arrived, Brooks has returned to the car with the headphones, gotten into the car where her son was safely and happily playing, and driven out of the parking lot—which, presumably the stranger had also witnessed—and by the time the police traced the car's plates to her parents' house, Brooks's flight had already left for Chicago. She learned all of this when she landed to a flurry of frantic calls and messages.

In the months that followed, Brooks consulted a lawyer and ultimately returned to Virginia to turn herself in for charges of child abandonment. In the aftermath of the incident, she recalled that "it seemed that every hope and good intention I'd had since becoming a mother had crumbled under the slightest pressure" (33-34). She writes that when she told friends about what had happened, they often asked some variation of the same question: how did you feel? She'd say "I was scared" or "I was shocked. . . ."

> And there was truth to all this. But the deeper truth was much worse. The deeper truth was that I felt as though I'd been caught doing something very bad, even if I didn't understand what the bad thing was, exactly, or what the rationale was for its badness. I felt, I think, what just about every woman feels whenever someone attacks or criticizes her mothering: I felt angry. I felt embarrassed. But beneath all that, I felt ashamed.

The trajectory from feeling shame to being isolated is straightforward. Brooks, a person who by her own description cannot keep a secret, began to closely guard the secret of the morning in the parking lot. As she learned more about the cultural forces behind the shame she was feeling and our society's deeply irrational anxiety around children left unattended in public places, she came to see much of our collective anxiety about children's safety as a misguided attempt at control. At one point, Brooks met Julie Koehler, a lawyer and a mother who returned from getting a cup of coffee to see a police officer harassing her three children she'd left waiting in the car. When Brooks asked Koehler "if she wasn't scared about a man driving a white van coming to snatch" her kids, she said no. "I don't worry about the man in the white van, and I'll tell you why. I'm a Cook County public defender. I have been for twenty years. And never in my twenty years of working there have I ever seen a single [stereotypical kidnapping] case. Not one. I've seen parents who abused their kids. I've seen parents who killed their children or whose relatives or spouses killed their children. But I work in the building where any case in Cook County would come if someone abducted a stranger's child, and there just aren't any. In twenty years, I have never seen a child abduction case." In explaining her own rationale for her decision to leave her son in the car, Brooks cites a 2014 statistic indicating "only .1 percent of missing person cases were what we'd think of as a 'stereotypical kidnapping' . . . abduction was simply not on the list of nightmare scenarios I worried about, and that list was long. But, I was rational in my hierarchy of fear" (32).

I'm not sure that any of us can truly be rational in a hierarchy of fear, but when I read *Small Animals* in the months after I left Simon in his stroller by the preschool playground, I was grateful for these statistics and mentally stored them away as antidotes to the profound sense of shame I'd shared with Brooks on the morning of my lapse in hyper-vigilance.

So much marketing of baby products is rooted in parental fear. In the same way that fear of terrorist attacks or political collapse or new coronavirus variants drives news ratings, fear of parental inadequacy is behind the near-fanatical research some parents conduct before making each baby purchase. When I spent the early spring of 2020 attached to my phone, constantly refreshing Covid-19 case trackers and scrolling Twitter for anecdotes about super-spreader events, when I woke anxiously in the middle of the night, what I was really afraid of was that something I could not control, had not even known to anticipate, was coming for the people I loved and that there might be nothing I could do to stop it. I imagined aerosolized particles, a term I was newly familiar with, blowing through our suburban yard, fat spiky droplets leftover from an uncovered cough on the outside of our milk gallon. It was in this same spirit that over the years I bought multiple sleep sacks, updating to new sizes when my babies outgrew the ones they were in and the reason some of my friends bought unreliable and expensive oxygen-monitoring booties to put on to their newborns while they slept. Writing for *The Verge* (the technology vertical at *Vox*), Katherine Boehret describes the Owlet, one such oxygen-monitoring device, and its marketing tactics:

[N]one of these is a medical device, nor can any be used to prevent Sudden Infant Death Syndrome, or SIDS. SIDS is every parent's worst nightmare. It accounted for

1,500 infant deaths in 2014 and remains unexplained and unpredictable.

Still, this doesn't stop companies from reminding parents what could happen if they don't buy in.

To see what I mean, try opening the website for Owlet, a $249.99 baby booty that uses pulse oximetry to monitor a kid's oxygen levels and heart rate. Before you can read anything about Owlet, the website immediately launches a video with three terrifying stories from mothers about how Owlet saved their children. The first mom says, "It started flashing red. I ran over there and unswaddled her. She was choking and she was blue around her mouth and nose." Another mom says, "One night it went off. I turned the lights on and noticed that he was blue around the mouth. I immediately stimulated him and he started breathing again."

It's not that precautions and safety awareness are foolish. Obviously many safety standards exist to protect consumers. My family and I wear helmets when we ride bikes, seatbelts in the car, replace our smoke detector batteries regularly. I'm not nostalgic for the days of unrestrained kids wrestling in the trunk of a station wagon or houses insulated with asbestos. A friend I dropped out of touch with years ago recently lost a baby at ten days. I saw the post she wrote on Facebook and wrote an anemic condolence; I have thought about her and her son every day since. I understand—and could alternately weep with despair and howl with rage at the knowledge—

that life is fragile. But there would be nothing protective in those howls or in my middle-of-the-night phone refreshing or the intrusive visions of strollers rolling down steps or off cliffs. It's tempting to behave as though my elevated heart rate and hyper-vigilance are themselves a means of keeping the most horrible thing I've ever known—that there is no guarantee that my children will be safe—at bay.

Hyper-vigilant, anxious, fear-based parenting comes at a cost to parents, to children, and more broadly, to society. There is the chance that more realistic risks (that a toddler might fall on crowded stairs, for example) are overshadowed by the risks that loom large and dramatic in the public imagination of parental failings like hot car deaths and kidnappings. Children face very real consequences from limited freedom and independence, and there is a profound emotional and social cost to parents. On the nights early in Thea's life when I slept with a video monitor next to our bed, the few hours between her night feedings passed in fitful nervous bouts of waking when she rolled over in her crib, starting when she grunted or cooed, and groggy grabs for my end of video monitor. When I realized that, a room away, I would hear her fine if she woke, that I could at least get some sleep while she did, I put the monitor away. Brooks sees our collective impulse to anxiety as originating not from any of the tangible fears these products, laws, or rituals are targeting, but from much a more profound and real fear about the future our children will inherit and our fundamental, if unspoken, understanding that we have very little control over the things that matter most in our children's lives— their future happiness, sense of worth, intellectual fulfillment, or protection from ravaging diseases. To give into this fear it is to lose quite a bit.

Like Brooks, Sarah Menkedick sees maternal fear as, at least in part, a symptom of isolation endured by so many new mothers and their children. In an early chapter of *Ordinary Insanity*, she points out that "the obsession with zero risk begins to engender a much bigger, unseen, unmeasured risk: the dramatic delimiting of women's lives by anxiety" (98), Reflecting candidly on her own experience with postpartum OCD, Menkedick goes on to suggest that "what is lost, thinking always of risk, aiming always for zero risk, is not measurable. There are no statistics, no charts, no metrics. There is a gecko in a cage with a heat lamp for a sun. There is a dog who has never been let off leash. There is no rain in the mouth. There is no solitude, no wandering to the edge of woods at dusk. There is no unwashed fruit eaten with dirty hands. There is no mess. There is no staking of oneself, one's small life, against the hugeness of the world. There is no sharing a meal with a stranger" (104).

Because both Thea and Simon were born in the darkest days of winter, I was widely encouraged to join a "mom's group." Our pediatric practice had one, which felt somehow less embarrassing than joining one I'd found on Facebook or on the bulletin board at the local library—as though I was there for medically-necessary, or at least medically-adjacent reasons. And I guess I was. In that room of strangers, I did meet some women who became true friends, but even those who merely became familiar faces provided a sense of community.

Our babies had all been born within a few weeks of one another. In these meetings we had the chance to ask the practice's lactation consultant questions about sleeping and swaddling and dry skin and nursing. Women mixed bottles of formula or put on nursing covers or pulled down their nursing tank tops without bothering. Babies cried and napped in car seats and afterwards we sometimes went to lunch at a mediocre American restaurant down the street where we propped the infant car seats in their travel-system frames or placed them gently at our feet and ate a meal with other women that we hadn't prepared and wouldn't have to clean up after. I always dreaded going but was always glad when I went.

For my first meeting, I chose my outfit carefully. Less than a week earlier, I had been 41 weeks and six days pregnant, so my choices were limited, but I also wanted to convey something about the self I'd been before I had children. I wore my loosest jeans and a plaid flannel shirt and my old gray converse sneakers. I thought the ideal outfit might suggest that I was a writer or the hint at the kind of music I listened to or how I'd voted in the most recent election, or at least that in another lifetime I had been a person who once went shopping for shoes. Until I had children the categories I belonged to were relatively narrow: long-distance runner, high school teacher, track coach, twice-failed vegetarian, writer. All of these parts of my identity were things I'd chosen but they were also things that I felt really said something about what mattered to me (or what did not matter enough to see through), about how I spent my days, about my strengths and weaknesses and the way I saw the world. So many people are parents that, although being a mother means more to me than any of these other things, I thought then that by itself being a mother indicated nothing about the specifics of the way I saw the world. I didn't yet see that having children did actually inform a great deal about how I'd see the world going forward, and so being part of a group whose only commonality was the age of our infants felt lonely and even superficial.

I can see now, though, that this, like many other groups of mothers I've witnessed or been involved with, was a concrete and meaningful community. Although it was one that has mostly dissolved as some of us moved or started new jobs or went back to work or got divorced, as our children grew older, more different from one another, as the questions we were navigating changed, it was also an important demonstration of something I hadn't yet understood to be universal. We had different lives outside of motherhood, different financial realities, different childcare situations, different career decisions to make, different strollers and maybe even different opinions on the very utility and morality of strollers—but we were all still bleeding and exhausted and frightened and anxious about the future our children would inherit.

In college, our assistant coach, Maggie, ran with us well into her third trimester. Online, I saw women calling themselves running bloggers or fitness influencers post pictures of their GPS watch data side-by-side with photographs of themselves smiling in profile, late-pregnancy belly protruding between running shorts and a sports bra like a neat basketball. Then after just a few weeks off post-delivery, the watch data was accompanied instead by a picture of them posing with or pushing a jogging stroller, complete with the heavy car seat attachment necessary to meet safety requirements for newborns. My friend Jen, who was already an accomplished runner pre-motherhood who'd raced for an NCAA Division I track and field program, ran personal best times in every event after having her first child and qualified for the U.S. Olympic trials between having her third and fourth. A woman who I knew for finishing well in front of me at local road races in the days before motherhood, when I was free to spend long weekend and after-work hours running mile after mile, used to boast about the daily 10-milers she logged pushing her youngest son in the running stroller while her older kids were at school. When I was pregnant with Thea, 10,000-meter world silver medalist Kara Goucher had just run 70-mile weeks through her pregnancy, and returned to racing when her son was just three months old. She'd gone on to finish fifth in the Boston Marathon in 2011 just six months postpartum. The time she ran, two hours, 24 minutes and 52 seconds—a pace of just over five and a half minutes per mile—was the fastest of her career. It seemed the only reason that becoming a mother would be the end to all my running would be if I were too lazy, too undisciplined to make training compatible with caring for young children.

In 2020 Nike launched a maternity clothing line with an aspirational series of advertisements featuring pregnant athletes and new mothers. After the ads began to air, it came to light—in what probably should not have been surprising—that Goucher, like many of Nike's other athletes, was working under exploitative contracts both during pregnancy (when she was unsalaried because she was not competing), and immediately postpartum when she was pressured to return to racing as quickly as possible. In 2021, Sarah Wassner Flynn covered the backlash to the ad campaign for *Triathlete* magazine, writing that "Goucher revealed that when she had her son, Colt, in 2010, she was told by Nike executives that she wouldn't be paid until she started racing again. . . . Back then, we celebrated her tenacity and her ability to rewrite the timeline on postpartum fitness. But, as Goucher later shared, the rushed return to competition in order to earn a paycheck resulted in a debilitating hip injury and took an emotional toll she still struggles with to this day."

In the months and years after Goucher became a mother, headlines like "Kara Goucher: Running, Being Mom Go Well Together," or "Goucher's Impressive Return to Fitness" celebrated her rapid return to world-class competition. But, years later, her husband remembered this time very differently:

Three months after giving birth, she was preparing to race a half marathon. In the days leading up to that race our son became seriously ill and was admitted to the hospital. In-between comforting our son, she would leave us at the hospital, guilt ridden and completely exhausted to go and train for her return to racing. The morning after our son was checked out of the hospital, he boarded a plane with us to Phoenix, AZ. Kara needed to race so she could stop the "clock ticking" on her return to racing. Needless to say her race did not go well. . . . All of this time there was no resolution with Nike for how long her suspension would last. In fact, Kara was in NYC racing a half marathon at the same time that she was pleading with the CEO of Nike, to understand her position. She was explaining the extreme stress, both physically and emotionally, this was causing her. She said she did not feel supported. While her sponsor had her splashed in ads, she was still not receiving a paycheck. She was told that as he understood it, her suspension was fair. We still have the emails showing that this conversation took place. When our son was 6 1/2 months old, Kara ran the Boston Marathon and placed 5th. She ran a PR 2:24. She was still under suspension (Goucher, Adam).

In interviews, Kara Goucher described lifting weights and running on the day she went into labor. At a minimum, women are advised to wait six weeks before returning to intense exercise; recent debate has suggested that 12 weeks would be a better marker. Goucher returned to training just two-and-a-half weeks postpartum, and then weaned her son earlier than she'd planned because logging 100-mile weeks while breastfeeding was unsustainable. Later, when her Nike coach Alberto Salazar was under investigation for anti-doping violations, Goucher told the BBC that he "had encouraged her to take the thyroid drug Cytomel to lose weight she'd gained during pregnancy" (Daly).

It's impossible for me, and I imagine for many serious distance runners, to mark where clear-eyed pragmatism about mass and velocity and the laws of physics—body weight and running speed—ends, and a more pathological anxiety about food and control begins. Unlike Kara Goucher, my livelihood has never depended on how fast I can run the 26 miles from Hopkinton to Boston, and so it also did not depend on if or how quickly I lost the weight I'd gained during pregnancy or if eating enough to maintain my milk supply meant that I carried a few additional pounds on my frame. But, I had, like almost all the women I know, internalized the message that it was important I lose pregnancy weight quickly, and that it was important I do so cheerfully, while breastfeeding, and without being away from my baby any more than I already had to be for work and the occasional marriage-sustaining date night. For all his baby-wearing evangelism, Dr. Sears does make an exception: a jogging stroller, he notes, is a great way to stay fit while spending time with your baby.

Everything I'd gleaned about motherhood in movies, television shows, magazines, and books since long before

I considered having children suggested that that my body would be irrevocably altered (hips misaligned, weight heavier, breasts and stomach saggier) by pregnancy. This was, I'd long understood, an obvious illustration of all the ways my life itself would be not just altered but damaged by motherhood and that it was my responsibility to be vigilant in returning my body to as close as I could to its pre-pregnancy size and shape. One way I could do this, I was reminded in pamphlets at the doctor's office and passages in pregnancy books, was to continue exercising through pregnancy.

It was only a half-mile, but I did get in one last run the morning before I had Thea. I'd switched to walking near the end of my pregnancy, but she was already ten days overdue and I thought a long walk followed by a short run might start labor (I don't think it did; my water broke late that night when I was checking in for a scheduled induction). Simon was a bigger baby, and running a five-mile Turkey Trot when I was 34 weeks pregnant with him made me unable to walk without grimacing in pain until I went into labor five weeks later. The pain—caused by what I later learned was a dislocated sacroiliac joint incurred by stubbornly plowing ahead so late in the third trimester—was so intense that I began to fantasize about going into labor just so I could have an epidural and feel relief from the pain radiating from where my pelvic bone met my lower back.

Both Simon and Thea were born in late December, and after those first few days of dizzying exhaustion, I felt intuitively that I had to get out during the short window I had of daylight hours. I'd been advised by parenting and pregnancy websites to wait until my baby was six weeks old and I was cleared by my midwife to resume any exercise more vigorous than walking, but both times I felt that to do so would come at great cost to my emotional and mental well-being. I didn't suffer from postpartum depression or anxiety, but could see how rapid and steep the descent into either might be if I did not go outside and do something that at that point in my life was at the core of my identity. When they were still too young to ride safely in the jogging stroller and I was not yet back coaching my high school athletes, I watched the sun sink lower in the sky as I waited for Nick to come home from work in time for me to leave the house, often for the first time that day, for a few quick miles. I was often unable to control my bladder on these runs, which I knew was a likely sign that my pelvic floor was not strong enough for running and might indicate a risk for serious complications like prolapse. That seemed a small price to pay for a daily sense of continuity with the person I'd been before having children.

By the time Thea went to kindergarten, I'd trained for three marathons since becoming a mother and had logged at least some of my training each time while pushing either the single or double running stroller. Yet, unlike the stroller-running rival I'd encountered at local road races, I never found a way to make more than a few miles enjoyable for me or my kids. The stroller slowed me down by about a minute a mile. More than 45 minutes of pushing the stroller left my back sore and my children cranky with confinement, but the short runs I did do with it made me stronger. I had to stand up straighter, use my upper body, particularly on hills. I chattered breathlessly, pointing out birds and bunnies and excavators and red houses and Little Free Libraries, fielded requests for

FIGURE 14 Amanda running with Thea in stroller.

water bottles and cheerios and ended runs at delis and ice cream shops and playgrounds. At the end of a summer spent pushing the stroller around at least a few times a week, I was stronger than I had been at the start, and running on my own felt like taking off a weighted vest. Slowing down, pushing the weight uphill, and then running free made me faster at 32, at 36, even at 38 than I'd been in those years when I had access to a college coaching staff, an athletic training room, and a teenager's body. It was a surprise and a thrill.

I talked with Abby Bales, a Doctor of Physical Therapy who is herself a marathon runner and mother of two young children. Her practice specializes in pelvic floor health and many of her patients are mothers, often who have been struggling with pelvic floor injuries for years after childbirth but haven't sought treatment for a complicated mix of reasons involving time, access, shame, and stigma. When her patients come to her with young children, Bales will often wear her patient's infant in a carrier while she treats the mother, or she'll make a home visit during nap time to accommodate her patient's schedule. She dreamed of offering on-site childcare, the way some gyms and fitness centers do, but the liability insurance for that would have been more expensive than the liability insurance for her medical practice.

One of Dr. Bales's core beliefs as a practitioner is that many women return to running too soon after birth. Running before they've rebuilt deep core strength and healed injuries from childbirth, compounded with hormonal changes postpartum, puts women at increased risk for a variety of both bone and soft-tissue injuries. When I asked her if she thinks using a running stroller increases those risks, she explained that pushing a stroller changes a runner's gait and creates a partially-closed chain that increases intra-abdominal pressure. For this reason, there are physiological reasons why she's concerned when she sees women running serious mileage with a stroller shortly after delivery. "It can be great for mental health, but as with all things postpartum you want to use it in moderation, starting with walking and making sure to slowly add" training. Even a light running stroller with a small baby weighs at least thirty-five pounds, and, a nursing mother is at already increased risk for Relative Energy Deficiency Syndrome (REDS, formerly known as the "female athlete triad" of amenorrhea, disordered eating, and excessive exercise).

Marketing a jogging stroller as a means of training for a marathon "in less than a year after delivery is very concerning . . . [B]oth the expectation that we 'should' be able to do this and that we are behind if we're not . . . is really pervasive in the running community," Bales explained. When I told her about my own mixed feelings, the way in which running with the stroller felt like a means of bringing my kids into a world I loved, the frustration I often had with the way the stroller slowed my pace and strained my back, and the recent nostalgia I'd been feeling knowing that those days are in the past, she was both sympathetic and pragmatic. "I had [a running stroller] because I needed it for my mental health, but there's a problem in our society and we keep creating products instead of supporting women. Products can't be in place of support or a community."

Sometimes when I was pushing Thea and Simon past the tennis courts and the baseball fields at our neighborhood park, we'd happen to pass a stroller fitness class underway. I'd often see women I knew from preschool or work or the pediatrician's new mom group participating. The instructors and many of the participants wore bright pink shirts with the group's logo. Although this group's website now boasts copy focused on self-care and instructors who "meet you where you are mentally and physically," an image, still available on Pinterest but no longer on the Fit4Mom.com website it originally came from, uses statistics about how many women gain more than the recommended 25-35 pounds during pregnancy. The site's original branding abounded with phrases like "get your body back" that I associated with the aims of postpartum fitness long before I ever considered having a child. In the new website copy, the phrase "no more mama guilt!" remains—but feels somehow more ambiguous. Is the guilt about weight? About working out apart from children? Or about not working out?

When I asked Bales about these groups, I expected her to mirror my mild disdain, if more professionally stated. Instead, citing how isolating motherhood, especially in the early years can be, she said, "those group classes, no matter what they are or how they're branded, if they're getting one of my moms out to be with other people outside of their babies, I'm supportive of it." Many women have no help and no community, she reminded me, and they're often going long stretches caring for their children without the help of partners, and feel shamed for hiring help or being away. As a result, Bales sees that women are "willing to destroy [their] bodies physically and mentally to rise to this standard that society is creating for us—that we can do it all." I thought, a little contrite, about how often I'd found the rush of feeling like I could "do it all" as intense as the rush of running a personal best or teaching a great class.

The difference in a woman nearing middle age who can run a five-kilometer race in nineteen minutes or eighteen minutes is, for all intents and purposes, insignificant. Both are good times for hobby runners and both are far from elite. Of course some of the thrill of bettering a past performance comes from the healthy and even admirable impulse to work toward a goal outside of career and family. But for me at least, some of that thrill is borne of a darker, more defensive, or even masochistic impulse where worth and work and suffering are all tied together.

Fitness communities are ripe for judgement and for cultishly insular devotion. Why, for example, do people buy candles scented like SoulCycle or hang flags representing their CrossFit gym on their homes? I know how annoying it is—even to me!—when marathon runners persist in wearing GPS watches out to dinner and talk with either too much or too little enthusiasm about food. But does my self-awareness about the neurotic and tedious aspects of running absolve me from bristling at the pink branding, the signaling of sorority-like community support, or the mid-burpees affirmations of Fit4Mom as I run past?

I feel all of the things this group presumably exists to address: desire to look like I did before I had children, the endorphin boost of exercise and fresh air, the support of a community of women, a way to achieve those things without paying for or coordinating childcare, and the vague, perhaps incorrect, but nevertheless stubborn belief that while there are a few things I truly cannot accomplish while caring for my awake young children (writing a book, for example), exercise is not one of them. Of course I can't race—or at least not to my full potential—while pushing a stroller, but I can go for a run.

Unlike Kara Goucher, who told ESPN that she never ran with a jogging stroller because training is her job, maximizing my performance is a luxury that I allow myself to seek out only in moderation—in the hours before the kids wake up, or on the weekends when Nick is home with them instead. On the days when I pushed the stroller in chilly temperatures nosy passersby told me were too cold, or when Simon or Thea complained through the last mile or fought over a jingle bell they'd been sharing, I felt defensive. I also felt, even on those days, heroic. Look what I'd done for myself and at no cost, or maybe even some gain, to them.

That tension—I think—is at the core of *no more mama guilt*. That it is possible to do something personally fulfilling without being a bad mother and that seeing their mothers do something personally fulfilling might in fact benefit children in subtle, wide-ranging ways that might not be as easy to quantify as the benefits of breastfeeding or baby-wearing or stroller safety are.

9 STROLLING

When L.N. screams that she *loves* her children and so would never push them away from her, she's acting out a deliberate caricature of a certain type of contemporary American mother, but she's also getting at the heart of one of parenthood's most painful, unsolvable contradictions: the balance between the imperative to protect and to push toward independence that I am always recalibrating. Putting my children in their own beds, coaxing them to sleep through the night, introducing them to solid food, sending them to school, teaching them to ride a bike, to swim, to read, to tie their own shoes, are all ways of pushing them away from me because I hope more than I've ever hoped for anything that they will one day in the very distant future live in this world we've shared after I'm gone and that when they do I will have taught them what they need to know.

In part 7 of her poem "Ultrasound," Scottish poet Kathleen Jamie writes:

Our baby's heart on the sixteen-week scan
was a fluttering bird, held in cupped hands.

I thought of St. Kevin, hands opened in prayer
and a bird of the hedgerow nesting there,

and how he'd borne it, until the young had flown
—and I prayed: this new heart must outlive my own.

According to Seamus Heaney's "St. Kevin and the Blackbird," St. Kevin is said to have, in extending a palm outside his narrow cell, provided a nestling place for a blackbird. "[M]oved to pity," Heaney writes, "he must now hold his hand/ Like a branch out in the sun and rain for weeks/ Until the young are hatched and fledged and flown."

Pushing a child in a stroller is an act of separation, but it's also an act of safe-guarding, and, as I recently began to worry when I walked through the neighborhood with four-year old Simon's long coltish legs dangling nearly to the ground, might not just be a portable little nest, safe but also, limiting, constrictive.

Jamie's essays and poetry about exploring the world with young children are the foundation for Melanie Duckworth's contemplative essay, "Everyone Wants to Escape from their Own Lives Sometimes, Don't They." In that piece, Duckworth reflects on the parallels and ruptures between the experiences of visiting London as a young, single woman and later as an academic with young children. "Twelve years ago, nearly to the day, I arrived in London with a huge backpack, a little backpack, and a brick of a laptop. I was brimming with excitement, anticipation, freedom, and nerves. Walking along the street, carrying it all, I felt like a giant turtle." Duckworth remembers the "grotty hostel" where she stayed, visits to the British Museum, and a mix of anxious, aimless wandering. "Last week," Duckworth writes, of a recent trip she took for an academic conference, "I arrived in London with Felix and Antonia as my companions. . . . We stayed in a clean and shiny hostel near Hyde Park."

Duckworth recalls that at the end of this second trip, "we walked from our apartment to the station to catch the train to Edinburgh. My big backpack was strapped to my back; the little backpack was slung over the handles of the stroller, where Antonia sat, as Felix walked beside me. When he got tired, he sat in the stroller and I strapped Antonia to my front in the baby carrier. We trundled slowly over the cobblestones like an oversized turtle. The train journey itself was less peaceful than I had anticipated, but there was a blissful moment when both children fell asleep on top of me until the conductor arrived and asked me to move my bags."

I know so well these less-peaceful-than-anticipated train rides and these blissful moments. Before Thea and Simon were in school, I loved to take them on adventures that exhausted all of us. A stranger once took a picture of us at Grand Central Station after a day at a children's art museum, lunch at a Pain Quotidien where Simon's stroller served as his high chair, many trips up and down subway stairs in which a stranger wordlessly grabbed one end of the stroller while I, then unaware of the risk of falling to my death or dropping

Simon to his, held the handles and hustled down to make the train. In the picture, one of my favorite photos, we are all exhausted, shimmering with sweat from a late-spring day in Manhattan, and waiting to board a commuter train bound for Connecticut on which I already planned to pull baggies

FIGURE 15 Amanda and kids in Grand Central Station.

of goldfish crackers and little milk cartons I'd been saving for late-day exhaustion out of my overstuffed diaper bag.

There is both joy and triumph in having shown the children I love so fiercely around the world I also love fiercely—a world of running, of exploring, of traveling, even of walking slowly through my neighborhood wondering how the new house down the block is coming along. In the best of cases, these stroller days felt like I'd managed to make a nest for my children, steady on a branch while still, through some magic, showing them the world. The exhaustion of these outings was not at odds with the joy and triumph I felt when we boarded the train home or I toweled off their little bodies, finally clean from all the dirt of the city or the running trail or the dusty corner of the playground. Traveling or running or exploring or navigating the world with them, no matter how hard, feels like triumph in its proof of my self-sufficiency and successful defiance of the expectation that motherhood would be an end to all of that. "Although motherhood restricts journeys," Duckworth notes, "it also enables and requires them—be they as simple as a walk to the bottom of the garden in the snow."

By the time Thea finished first grade, we were down to one stroller. The first to go had been the travel system; once Simon outgrew his infant car seat, it was useless, and, apparently these are so ubiquitous and the one I had so unremarkable that it took weeks before I could even give it away. I sold the double-BOB for $50 on a neighborhood tag sale page, thinking that with Thea in school I'd have no use for it (when the pandemic closed schools, I regretted that decision). I donated the heavy, unwieldy two-child stroller I'd pushed all over Manhattan and Brooklyn when it became clear that by the time we'd be traveling again, we'd have no need for it.

On an icy morning in February, I was hurrying to drop Thea off at her elementary school and bring Simon on to his preschool. I'd loaded him in the single running stroller to save time and help him safely navigate the lingering icy patches on the sidewalk. A jagged patch of refrozen slush caught the edge of the rear right tire and shredded it open. I pushed him in the stroller with the flat tire for the rest of our commute, but when I got it home and took a closer look, I saw that at the very least the tire and tube would need to be replaced. This stroller, the one my parents bought me when I was pregnant with Thea, was so dirty, missing so many pieces (its canopy, its cup holder, a piece that made the straps adjust for different-sized children) that there was no sense in selling or even donating it, so I put it on the curb for garbage collection the next Thursday morning.

Simon is too big for our remaining stroller, but occasionally I use it anyway. We live far enough from his school that at the end of a hot June day, it's sometimes hard for him to make the walk home. Sometimes I think—or maybe just imagine— that I see other parents of a more sporty variety, the kind whose children learned to swim at two and ride two-wheelers at three and play lacrosse at four and who have not been so passively perambulated since toddlerhood, giving me a look, judging me in the way I imagined the UPPABaby VISTA parents judging me (or knew myself to be judging them).

But I love these walks with Simon, the pace of our perambulating so different from any other pace in my life. Slower than driving, biking, running and even than the clip at which I'd walk on my own, but still faster and more even than the erratic pace Simon and I keep when, holding hands, running late, arriving just in time for the late bell we hustle down the sidewalk stroller-less. On the stroller walks, we have time to consider the houses we pass, the flags we see flying, the construction vehicles at work. In the last weeks of the public school year, we often passed parents and what looked to be college students newly arrived home for their summer vacation. Often, the parent and I made eye contact, a silent and almost mournful recognition passing between us.

In June, just as I'd started working on this book, I was finishing up an early-morning run when I passed a mother pushing her double-BOB running stroller past the park across the street from the little in-home preschool both Thea and Simon attended the years they were two. Her children looked to have about the same number of years between them as mine. Her daughter was about the age Thea was at the end of the school year when she attended that preschool, and her son, like Simon had been then, still a baby, big enough to sit up but probably not yet crawling.

I felt a pang of nostalgia so intense that knowing it was rooted in romanticization of those years did nothing to ease its ache. I imagined a whole life for this woman—a husband traveling for work for ten days and nine nights, trying to fit in training for an upcoming half marathon without childcare and children who rose before dawn—that I realized only later was a replica of the precise circumstance I'd been in when the sun was rising at just this hour, when the late-spring weather was humid just like this. In my own real-life version of those two weeks, I felt heroic when Nick returned. I had run every single day he was gone, and only once with help from my parents (who would gladly have helped more). We'd gone to playgrounds and I'd orchestrated simultaneous naps so that I could meet my first major freelance deadline. We'd eaten ice cream for dinner and hosted my long-time friend on a visit from Manhattan. After Thea and Simon were in bed, I'd watched the entire series of *Big Little Lies* before my free HBO trial ran out. Even with Nick away, I'd run and written and seen friends and watched adult television. Motherhood had not been an end to all that—to me.

That stretch of days had been hard but it had been brief, and, it had been easy in some important ways. The kids were young enough still to be strapped in, to nap reliably each day, to find magic in the vine-covered public easement that runs between the senior center and the town dump. I had been able to keep them with me everywhere I went and to do, at least for a short time, everything I needed to get done. It was slower or slightly more encumbered, but it also felt somehow more significant. In the most literal sense, running with the stroller for all those days leading up to my half marathon made the race itself, which I ran without the stroller, feel easy by comparison. The pre-dawn hours I spent on my couch finishing my essay made a creative life feel like something

I had the power to mine and cultivate, even with, or maybe because of, the pram in the hall.

It wasn't all like that, of course. Not that stretch of specific days and more generally not that phase of life: when I was so sleep-deprived that I frequently walked into walls, or when I was breastfeeding one child while sitting on the floor of our half-bathroom potty-training the other; when I felt often that my entire identity had been deconstructed and I had not yet found a way to reassemble it; when the physical demands of motherhood and their differences from fatherhood felt most stark and sometimes led to the darkest of marital resentment and discord.

But, I missed Thea and Simon very much as I ran past that double stroller, both the six and four-year-olds I'd left sleeping at home when I laced up my shoes that morning and the two-year-old girl and baby boy who, no matter how much I'd tried to record and how many iPhone pictures I'd taken, were becoming ever-more hazy memories.

The days of hot mornings pushing a stroller had also been days of baby music class, months when the parenting choices I made were manageable and concrete: what kind of soap would be gentler on sensitive infant skin? If there was whining in line for ice cream, should we leave right away or should I first give a stern warning? The things my children needed from me were mostly things I was able to give them, and they were rarely without me, even when I was running. I lived my life not separately from theirs, the way even in early elementary school it has already become possible with long school days and drop-off play dates, but fitted neatly in the spaces where naps and preschool allowed.

Our stroller—our many strollers, I guess I should say—made it possible for parenting young children to be exactly what I feared was impossible. I could bring Thea and Simon with me on the adventures I loved most of all. I pushed Thea on trails cut through a meadow at an old estate where I'd once coached and raced cross country meets. It was slower and more awkward and sometimes uncoordinated or even briefly frustrating, but on a sunny fall morning I'd done something I loved in a place I loved with a person I loved. The same was true of the subway treks and the Brooklyn Bridge walks and even the TriBeCa playground. I'd never have thought to spend time on an early Sunday morning at a TriBeCa playground, but I was outside with my family, eating an almond croissant and drinking an iced coffee, people watching, puzzling over how to make sense of where I fit in and didn't, just like I've been doing in various ways and places since I was a child myself.

The moments of self-consciousness about my dirty stroller, by the end showing spots of mold on its canopy, next to the UPPABaby VISTAs, have been balanced by the sense I often have that all these miles my kids and I have traversed together have changed us. Thea will be seven soon, and I think often of the lore about all the cells in our body regenerating in that period of time as a neat match to the image I have of the tires rubbed bald from training runs and playground trips and travel I've shared with my children.

A TAXONOMY OF STROLLER AS METAPHOR

1. Stroller as metaphor

    a. Consumption as care: marketing to expecting
        and new parents assumes a shared belief
        that the right stroller with the right safety
        requirements will both safeguard against injury
        and signal parental devotion and vigilance

    b. Inevitability of danger: particularly alarming
        for the literal dangers inherent in a product
        designed to keep children safe and the
        horrifying combination of innocence and the
        threat of violence

    c. Sombre threat to creativity: the phrase English
        literary critic Cyril used to describe the effect of
        parenthood (the pram in the hall) on art

d. Convenience-granting encumbrance: walking, running, navigating busy airports is easier—mostly—but also requires avoiding stairs, going slower, and making wide turns

e. Pushing away while keeping close: a typical stroller provides a balance that is elsewhere painfully elusive in parenthood: children have the independence that comes from being at a distance, looking out at the world, yet even as they are being pushed away, they remain are in the safety of arm's reach

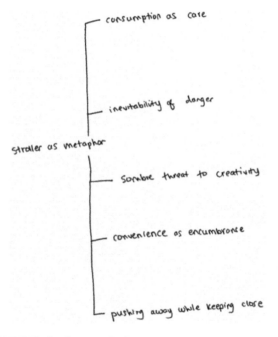

FIGURE 16 Stroller as metaphor.

WORKS CITED

Bales, Abby. Phone interview. Conducted by Amanda Morgan June 28, 2021.

Boehret, Katherine. "Baby Tech Is Sold on Fear, Not Practicality." *The Verge*, The Verge, March 11, 2016, www.theverge.com/tech /2016/3/11/11204234/Baby-tech-sold-fear-practicality-parent -buying.

Boyce, Frank Cottrell. "The Parent Trap: Art after Children." *The Guardian*, Guardian News and Media, August 1, 2010, https:// www.theguardian.com/culture/2010/aug/01/art-children-pram -hallway.

Brooks, Kim. *Small Animals: Parenthood in the Age of Fear*. United States, Flatiron Books, 2018.

Broude, Norma. "Mary Cassatt: Modern Woman or the Cult of True Womanhood?" *Woman's Art Journal*, vol. 21, no. 2, 2000, pp. 36–43. *JSTOR*, www.jstor.org/stable/1358749. Accessed July 20, 2021.

Cassatt, Mary. *Children in a Garden (The Nurse)*. 1878, Museum of Fine Arts, Houston, USA.

Daly, Mark. "Top Athletics Coach Alberto Salazar Faces Doping Claims." *BBC News*, BBC, June 3, 2015, www.bbc.com/news/uk -scotland-32877702.

Doyle, Roddy. *The Deportees*. United States, Viking Books, 2007.

Druckerman, Pamela. *Bringing Up Bébé: One American Woman Discovers the Wisdom of French Parenting.* United States, Penguin Books, 2014.

Duckworth, Melanie. ""Everyone Wants to Escape from their Own Lives Sometimes, Don't They." *Travellin Mama: Mothers, Mothering and Travel.* Beyer, Charlotte, ed. Canada, Demeter Press, 2019.

Eldridge, Sarah. Email interview. Conducted by Amanda Morgan June 15, 2021 and June 18, 2021.

Fisher, Michelle Millar and Winick, Amber. *Designing Motherhood.* United States, MIT Press, 2021.

Ferguson, Molly E. "Reading the Ghost Story: Roddy Doyle's 'The Deportees and Other Stories.'" *The Canadian Journal of Irish Studies*, vol. 35, no. 2, 2009, pp. 52–60. *JSTOR*, www.jstor.org/stable/41415002. Accessed July 20, 2021.

"Fitness For Moms - FIT4MOM Southeast Fairfield County." Southeast Fairfield County, seffco.fit4mom.com/.

Flynn, Sarah Wassner."No One Should Ever Be Penalized for Getting Pregnant.'" *Triathlete*, April 2, 2021, www.triathlete.com/culture/no-one-should-ever-be-penalized-for-getting-pregnant/.

Gardner, Lyn. "The Pram in the Hall Is No Enemy of Good Art – It Inspires Great Theatre." *The Guardian*, Guardian News and Media, February 8, 2018, https://www.theguardian.com/stage/2018/feb/08/pram-in-the-hallway-art-frances-poet-monica-dolan-theatre.

Gill, John Freeman. "The Land of the $800 Stroller." *The New York Times*, May 6, 2011, www.nytimes.com/2011/05/08/realestate/08living.html.

Goucher, Adam. "It's Time for Me to Use My Voice." *Podium Retreats*, retreat.karagoucher.com/its-time-for-me-to-use-my-voice/.

Heaney, Seamus. "St Kevin and the Blackbird." *Poetry Archive*, December 11, 2019, poetryarchive.org/poem/st-kevin-and-blackbird/.

Hesse, Monica "The Unreasonable Expectations of American Motherhood." *The Washington Post*, June 15, 2021.

Ingle, Robin, et al "Injuries Associated with Strollers," Washington DC, U.S. Consumer Product Safety Commission, 2000.

Jamie, Kathleen. "Ultrasound," *Waterlight: Selected Poems*. Minneapolis, MN, 1999.

Jones, Shane. "The Pram in the Hall." *The Paris Review*, January 30, 2014, https://www.theparisreview.org/blog/2014/01/29/the-pram-in-the-hall/.

Kampman, Wendy. Email interview. Conducted by Amanda Morgan, July 5, 2021.

"Kate Middleton Will Be Pushing Royal Baby 3 in This Carriage." *Architectural Digest*, Architectural Digest, April 23, 2018, www.architecturaldigest.com/story/kate-middleton-will-be-pushing-royal-baby-3-in-this-carriage.

Keystone. "A Gas Masked Young Mother Attends to Her Child's Pram Gas Mask during . . ." *Getty Images*, www.gettyimages.co.uk/detail/news-photo/gas-masked-young-mother-attends-to-her-childs-pram-gas-mask-news-photo/3319390.

"Kids," *Farfetch*, accessed July 15, 2021

Mendes, Sam, et al. *Away We Go*. Focus Features, 2009.

Menkedick, Sarah. *Ordinary Insanity: Fear and the Silent Crisis of Motherhood in America*. United States, Pantheon, 2019.

Merritt, Stephanie and Rogers, Jude. "Is the Pram in the Hall Still the Enemy of Good Art?" The Guardian, Guardian News and Media, June 20, 2015, https://www.theguardian.com/commentisfree/2015/jun/20/is-pram-in-hall-enemy-good-art-debate-cyril-connolly-bbc-artsnight.

O'Hehir, Andrew. "How 'Battleship Potemkin' Reshaped Hollywood." *Salon*, Salon.com, September 25, 2011, www.salon.com/2011/01/12/potemkin/.

"Perambulator: V&A Explore The Collections." *Victoria and Albert Museum: Explore the Collections*, collections.vam.ac.uk/item/O176087/perambulator-alfons-pollak/.

Sewell, Samuel J. "The History of Children's and Invalids' Carriages." *Journal of the Royal Society of Arts*, vol. 71, no. 3694, 1923, pp. 716–728. *JSTOR*, www.jstor.org/stable/41356294. Accessed July 15, 2021.

Silverman, Leah. "All 3 Royal Babies Left the Hospital in This $75 Wool Shawl." *Town & Country*, Town & Country, March 3, 2021, www.townandcountrymag.com/style/home-decor/ g19596276/kate-middleton-prince-william-favorite-baby -brands/.

Taylor, Janelle S. "Of Sonograms and Baby Prams: Prenatal Diagnosis, Pregnancy, and Consumption." *Feminist Studies*, vol. 26, no. 2, 2000, pp. 391–418. *JSTOR*, www.jstor.org/stable /3178541. Accessed July 15, 2021.

"Vista." *UppaBaby*, accessed July 15, 2021

Wax, Emily "'In Africa We Carry Our Children so They Feel Loved'." *The Guardian*, Guardian News and Media, June 18, 2004, www.theguardian.com/theguardian/2004/jun/18/ guardianweekly.guardianweekly12.

Wingate, Steven. "Quotes & Notes: The Pram in the Hall." *Fiction Writers Review*, https://fictionwritersreview.com/shoptalk/ quotes-notes-the-pram-in-the-hall/.

"White House--Major Russell Harrison and Harrison Children-- Baby McKee and Sister on Goat Cart." *The Library of Congress*, www.loc.gov/item/97510241/.

Wyndham, Aradia. "From Baby Toting to Babywearing." *The Baby Historian*, September 21, 2019, thebabyhistorian.com/2016/10 /27/from-baby-toting-to-babywearing/.

ACKNOWLEDGMENTS

I have dreamed of writing a book since I was a little girl, and neither that dream nor this specific book would have been possible without all kinds of support from all kinds of people.

Thank you to Object Lessons editors, Chris Schaberg (one of the only editors I've encountered who told me to take *more* stylistic risks, for which I am so grateful) and Ian Bogost, and the rest of the team at Bloomsbury: Haaris Naqvi, Rachel Moore (of unending patience with my many questions!), Zeba Talkhani, Christina Kowalski, Dhanuja Ravi, Anahi Molina, Nivethitha Tamilselvan, Nina Hayes-Thompson, and Mollie Broad. Alice Marwick, the cover artwork is perfect.

So much of this book relied on friends who generously shared ideas and experiences. Sarah Eldridge, Wendy Kampman, Abby Bales, Emily Delaney, Clarisse Mesa, Jenny Ingram—thank you for all your insights. The work of Kim Brooks, Sarah Menkedick, and Amber Winick, and Michelle Millar Fisher are at the core of how I began to see what I'd anecdotally observed about stroller culture as part of something bigger.

Thank you to friends and family who kindly read early chapters: Arielle Bernstein, the most generous of writing friends, Clay Parrish, Abby Lorge, Dylan Walsh, and Diane Parrish. Thank you to T Kira Madden's Lighthouse Writers Workshop for letting me cry happy tears over Zoom on the day I signed my contract, to my wonderful agent Jackie Gilbert for answering a million questions and sharing a million running miles, and to my always supportive colleagues at the Westport Writers' Workshop and Fairfield University.

I've been lucky to find, in suburban Connecticut of all places, a group of fiercely loyal fellow travelers who have watched my children, listened to me ramble about strollers, and celebrated this project with me at every step in the process. Thank you, friends.

In 9th grade, my English teacher, Calvin Burwell, told me I'd have to dedicate my first book to him, and, all these years later, I am.

My parents, Diane and Steve Parrish, encouraged me to write from before I could hold a pencil. My dad transcribed my first story (Poopy Ducky, 1985) and my mom took me to my first literary event (Ann M. Martin, 1991). Thank you for being my lifelong first readers, most unwavering supporters, and the purveyors of our two most heavily used strollers.

My sweet little family: Nick, I could, for so many reasons, not have done this without you. Thank you for making this two-ring parenting-writing circus possible. Thea and Simon, I wrote this book for you and because of you and, although, I didn't realize it at the time, it's also been a way preserve moments of sublime tenderness in the daily work of pushing away and keeping close.

INDEX

OBJECT LESSONS

Cross them all off your list.

9781501358159   9781501353277   9781501348716

9781501353024   9781501344350   9781501361906

> ## "Perfect for slipping in a pocket and pulling out when life is on hold."
> – *Toronto Star*

bird
ERIK ANDERSON

9781501353352

cell tower
STEVEN E. JONES

9781501348815

compact disc
ROBERT BARRY

9781501348518

ocean
STEVE MENTZ

9781501348631

high heel
SUMMER BRENNAN

9781501325991

hood
ALISON KINNEY

9781501307409

Blackface

Examines Hollywood's painful, enduring ties to racist performances"

—*Variety*

Sharp ... In explicitly laying out the history and costs of blackface performance, [Ayanna Thompson] fully meets her stated aim of offering an accessible book that constitutes part of an ongoing 'arc toward justice."

—*Times Higher Education*

Wide-ranging and hard-hitting ... a passionate, well-informed, and gripping read ... another triumph for *Object Lessons*."

—*New York Journal of Books*

Sticker

> Hoke (*The Groundhog Forever*) offers up an evocative reflection on queerness, race, and his hometown of Charlottesville, Va., in this conceptual 'memoir in 20 stickers.' Part of Bloomsbury's *Object Lessons* series, his book uses the humble sticker as a metaphorical linchpin for a series of essays that [offer] a unique perspective on one of the most infamous cities in recent American history."
>
> —*Publishers Weekly*

> We're not entirely objective here, but we're quite fond of the *Object Lessons* series—and Henry Hoke's contribution might boast the most striking cover design the series has had to date. Hoke's book uses stickers to chronicle everything from queer identity to the recent history of Charlottesville, Virginia—all of which should make this a book that sticks with you long after you've read it. (Pun intended, oh yes.)"
>
> —*Volume I Brooklyn*

Spacecraft

It's a story born of a specific cultural imaginary common among children of the last decades of the previous century ... *Spacecraft*, then, is a vehicle in which Morton meditates on futurality. The Millennium Falcon, along with hyperspace, is at the center of this meditation."

—*3 Quarks Daily*

Burger

Based on meticulous, and comprehensive, research, Adams has packed a stunning, gripping expose into these few pages – one that may make you rethink your relationship with this food. Five stars."

—*San Francisco Book Review*

Adams would seem the least likely person to write about hamburgers with her philosophically lurid antipathy to carnivory. But if the point is to deconstruct this iconic all-American meal, then she is the woman for the job."

—*Times Higher Education*

High Heel

A kaleidoscopic view of feminine public existence, both wide-ranging and thoughtful."

—*Jezebel*

From Cinderella's glass slippers to Carrie Bradshaw's Manolo Blahniks, Summer Brennan deftly analyzes one of the world's most provocative and sexualized fashion accessories ... Whether you see high heels as empowering or a submission to patriarchal gender roles (or land somewhere in between), you'll likely never look at a pair the same way again after reading *High Heel*."

—*Longreads*

Brennan's book, written in very small sections, is short, but powerful enough to completely change your world view."

—*Refinery29*

Hood

> Provocative and highly informative, Alison Kinney's *Hood* considers this seemingly neutral garment accessory and reveals it to be vexed by a long history of violence, from the Grim Reaper to the KKK and beyond-a history we would do well to address, and redress. Readers will never see hoods the same way again."

— Sister Helen Prejean, author of *Dead Man Walking*

> *Hood* is searing. It describes the historical properties of the hood, but focuses on this object's modern-day connotations. Notably, it dissects the racial fear evoked by young black men in hoodies, as shown by the senseless killings of unarmed black males. It also touches on U.S. service members' use of hoods to mock and torture prisoners at Abu Ghraib. Hoods can represent the (sometimes toxic) power of secret affiliations, from monks to Ku Klux Klan members. And clearly they can also be used by those in power to dehumanize others. In short, *Hood* does an excellent job of unspooling the many faces of hoods."

— *Book Riot*

[*Hood*] is part of a series entitled Object Lessons, which looks at 'the hidden lives of ordinary things' and which are all utterly 'Fridge Brilliant' (defined by TV Tropes as an experience of sudden revelation, like the light coming on when you open a refrigerator door). ... In many ways *Hood* isn't about hoods at all. It's about what – and who – is under the hood. It's about the hooding, the hooders and the hoodees ... [and] identity, power and politics. ... Kinney's book certainly reveals the complex history of the hood in America."

—*London Review of Books*

Personal Stereo:

[Rebecca Tuhus-Dubrow's] thoughtfulness imbues this chronicle of a once-modern, now-obsolete device with a mindfulness that isn't often seen in writing about technology."

—*Pitchfork* (named one of *Pitchfork*'s favorite books of 2017)

After finishing *Personal Stereo*, I found myself wondering about the secret lives of every object around me, as if each device were whispering, 'Oh, I am much so more than meets the eye'... Tuhus-Dubrow is a master researcher and synthesizer. ... *Personal Stereo* is a joy to read."

—*Los Angeles Review of Books*

Souvenir

Rolf Potts writes with the soul of an explorer and a scholar's love of research. Much like the objects that we bestow with meaning, this book carries a rich, lingering resonance. A gem."

—Andrew McCarthy, actor, director, and author of *The Longest Way Home* (2013)

A treasure trove of … fascinating deep dives into the history of travel keepsakes … Potts walks us through the origins of some of the most popular vacation memorabilia, including postcards and the still confoundedly ubiquitous souvenir spoons. He also examines the history of the more somber side of mementos, those depicting crimes and tragedies. Overall, the book, as do souvenirs themselves, speaks to the broader issues of time, memory, adventure, and nostalgia."

—*The Boston Globe*

Veil

Slim but formidable."

—*London Review of Books*

Rafia Zakaria's Veil shifts the balance away from white
secular Europe toward the experience of Muslim
women, mapping the stereotypical representations of
the veil in Western culture and then reflecting, in an
intensely personal way, on the many meanings that
the veil can have for the people who wear it . . . [*Veil*
is] useful and important, providing needed insight
and detail to deepen our understanding of how we got
here—a necessary step for thinking about whether and
how we might be able to move to a better place."

—*The Nation*

An intellectually bracing, beautifully written exploration
of an item of clothing all too freighted with meaning."

—Molly Crabapple, artist, journalist, and
author of *Drawing Blood (2015)*